SERVE YOURSELF

SERVE
YOURSELF

NIGHTLY ADVENTURES IN COOKING FOR ONE

Ten Speed Press and the Ten Speed Press colophon are registered
trademarks of Random House, Inc.

Library of Congress Cataloging-in-Publication Data

Yonan, Joe.
  Serve yourself : nightly adventures in cooking for one / Joe Yonan.
      p. cm.
  1. Cooking for one. 2. Cookbooks. I. Title.
  TX652.Y68 2011
  641.5'611—dc22
                                    2010040639

ISBN 978-1-58008-513-7

Printed in China

Design by Ed Anderson
Production by Colleen Cain

10 9 8 7 6 5 4 3 2 1

First Edition

For Mom, whose ease in the kitchen inspired my own.

CONTENTS

Preface x

Acknowledgments xiii

Pickled Anchos 20

Essay
Réservation pour Un 24

CHAPTER 1
BASIC RECIPES, CONDIMENTS, AND PICKLES

12-Hour Tomatoes 2

Corn Broth 3

Herbed Lemon Confit 4

Spicy Hummus 5

Mulled Wine Syrup 6

Cashew Tamari Dressing 7

Parsley Garlic Dressing 8

Cilantro Vinaigrette 9

Blueberry Lemon Jam 10

Strawberry Vanilla Jam 12

Salsa Verde 14

Blackened Salsa 16

Red Pepper Chutney 17

Cabbage and Pear Kimchi 18

Citrus-Pickled Onions 19

CHAPTER 2
EGGS

Benedict Rancheros 29

Low, Slow, and Custardy Eggs 30

Mushroom and Green Garlic Frittata 32

Baked Egg in Fall Vegetables 33

Swiss Chard, Bacon, and Goat
Cheese Omelet 34

Shrimp and Potato Chip Tortilla 35

Puffy Duck Egg Frittata
with Smoked Salmon 36

CHAPTER 3
SWEET POTATOES, BEANS, AND OTHER VEGGIES

Sweet Potato Soup Base 41

Sweet Potato Soup with Chorizo,
Chickpeas, and Kale 43

Sweet Potato and Orange Soup
with Smoky Pecans 44

Miso Pork on a Sweet Potato	45	Chili Cheese Enchiladas	64
Curried Shrimp on a Sweet Potato	46	Spicy Glazed Mini Meatloaf	65
Home-Cooked Beans	47	Yucatan-Style Slow-Roasted Pork	66
Roasted Chile Relleno with Avocado-Chipotle Sauce	48	Pork Chop with Apples and Brussels Sprouts	68
Peasant's Bowl	50	Essay First, Kill Your Chicken	69
Ex-Texas Salad	51		
Spicy Black Bean Soup Base	52	Roast Chicken Leg with Gremolata and Sunchokes	72
Black Bean Tortilla Soup with Shrimp and Corn	53	Pineapple-Juice-Can Hen and Baby Potatoes	74
Black Bean Soup with Seared Scallops and Green Salsa	54	Wine-Braised Chicken Thighs with Olives, Prunes, and Almonds	76
Stewed Cauliflower, Butternut Squash, and Tomatoes	55	Cornish Hen with Cherry-Hazelnut Wine Sauce	77
Warm Spinach Salad with Shiitakes, Corn, and Bacon	56	Mahi Mahi with Kiwi-Avocado Salsa and Coconut Rice	79
Fall Vegetable Soup with White Beans	58	Turbot with Tomatoes, Walnuts, and Capers over Couscous	80
		Gingery Glazed Halibut with Carrots and Baby Bok Choy	81

CHAPTER 4
MEAT, POULTRY, AND SEAFOOD

Essay Deep in the Heart of Texas, We Bread Steak	60		
Pan-Fried Sirloin with Smashed Potatoes and Anchovy Sauce	62		
Texas Bowl o' Red	63		

CHAPTER 5
TACOS

Homemade Corn Tortillas	84		
Austin-Style Breakfast Tacos	86		

Tacos de Huevos   87

Tacos with Mushrooms and   88
Chili-Caramelized Onions

Chickpea, Spinach, Feta,   89
and Pepita Tacos

Pastoral Tacos   91

Korean Short Rib Tacos   92

Cochinita Pibil Tacos   95
with Habanero Salsa

Smoked Turkey Tacos with Mole Verde   96

Duck Breast Tacos with Plum Salsa   99

Catfish Tacos with Chipotle Slaw   101

Shrimp Tacos with Grapefruit–   102
Black Bean Salsa

Smoked Trout, Potato, and Fennel Pizza   113

Eggplant and Spicy Hummus Flatbread   115

Three-Pepper Pizza with Goat Cheese   118

CHAPTER 7
SANDWICHES

Pulled Pork Sandwich   121
with Green Mango Slaw

Gingered Chicken Sandwich   122
with Avocado and Mango

Tuna, Egg, and Potato Salad Sandwich   123

Philly-Style Chicken Cutlet Sandwich   125

Tuna, Chickpea, and Arugula Sandwich   126

Avocado, Smoked Oyster,   127
and Pistachio Bruschetta

Smoked Trout, Green Apple,   128
and Gouda Sandwich

CHAPTER 6
PIZZA

No-Knead Pizza Dough   104

No-Knead Pizza Dough with Spelt   105

Smoky Pizza Margherita   106

Kimchi, Ham, and Fried Egg Pizza   107

Mushroom and Speck Pizza   109

Fig, Taleggio, and Radicchio Pizza   111

CHAPTER 8
RICE, GRAINS, AND PASTA

Thai Fried Rice with Runny Egg   132

Corn Risotto with Roasted   135
Cherry Tomatoes

Fried Rice with Cauliflower and Kimchi 136

Curried Butternut Squash Risotto 137

Personal Paella with Squid
and Scallions 139

Faux-lognese with Pappardelle 140

Farfalle with Cantaloupe
and Prosciutto 141

Farro Salad with Chickpeas, Cherries,
and Pecans 143

Charred Asparagus, Tofu,
and Farro Salad 144

Miso Mac and Cheese with Mushrooms 145

Spicy Almond Soba Noodles
with Edamame 147

Fedelini with Tuna Ragu 148

Fideos with Sardines
and Bread Crumbs 149

Cappuccino Tapioca Pudding
with Cardamom Brûlée 157

Hibiscus-Poached Peach 158

Spicy Coconut Sorbet 159

Yogurt Parfait with Rhubarb-Ginger
Sauce and Strawberries 160

Yogurt Parfait with Mulled Red Wine
Syrup, Oranges, and Almonds 161

Coconut French Toast
with Bananas Foster 162

Cherry-Almond Tart 163

Blueberry-Lemon Tart
with Toasted Coconut 165

Essay
Cooking for Two 166

Index 170

CHAPTER 9
DESSERTS

No-Bake Chocolate Oat Cookies 152

Cardamom–Brown Sugar
Snickerdoodles 153

Pistachio Butter Cookies 154

PREFACE

It was a Facebook comment that finally did it.

I had just posted a link to one of my "Cooking for One" columns in *The Washington Post*, and amid the compliments on the recipes for mulled wine syrup and salmon braised in Pinot Noir, I got this: "At the risk of getting too personal, perhaps you might find someone to share life/meals with. That would kill your column concept, but could change your life in a positive way. The pleasures of the table are so satisfying when shared."

Well, of course they are, and I share them all the time. A few days earlier, I had paid up on a promised birthday meal for two friends by kneading flour and egg until it was smooth as baby's skin, running it through thinner and thinner settings on a pasta machine, and hand-cutting it into pappardelle. I served it with a ragu bianca: chicken thighs ground with chicken livers, simmered in white wine, and tossed with olive oil and shaved pecorino. We scarfed down the silky noodles and the deeply flavored sauce and sipped Cabernet while toasting to another year and the impending approval of my Canadian friend's green card application.

I fold candied ginger and lemon juice into pound cake batter, bake it until barely done, glaze it with more ginger and lemon, then take it to dinner-party hosts. Extra batches of some cookie experiment go to colleagues at work. I butterfly one of my sister's homegrown turkeys, set it over dressing, and blast it in her 800°F brick bread oven for Thanksgiving in Maine. And when I'm dating, I'll court the object of my affection by stuffing a chicken with kaffir lime leaves and roasting it over sweet potatoes, then rolling homemade grapefruit curd and blackberries inside freshly made crepes.

Or, I dine out with friends, trying a Viognier with avocado-pistachio bruschetta at a hot new wine bar or marveling at the liquefied olives at a six-seat temple to molecular gastronomy. And sometimes, naturally, I'm so angry and hungry at the end of a workday (a combination I call "hangry") that it's all I can do to grab a falafel on the way home, or dial up the nearest Chinese restaurant for delivery that's so speedy it makes me wonder if they're stir-frying in my basement.

But those are all exceptions. The every night rule is a meal that's all about me, start to finish, and I keep all the pleasures of the table to myself. And why wouldn't I? Not to break into "The Greatest Love of All" about it or anything, but to me, cooking is the ultimate act of self-appreciation. When I cook for myself, I tend to make something more off-the-cuff, a little less refined than I make for friends, but I always strive for something sustaining, even energizing. Not only do I want (and of course need) to eat, but I also like to do it in a way that satisfies me on every level. It's partly that I want to have control over what I eat, but it's also about answering my particular, ever-shifting cravings. After all, only I really know what I want, and I usually know how to make it. If I don't, I'm willing to learn, and that confidence has formed the basis of my cooking explorations for most of my life.

The Facebook comment was innocent enough, I guess; but frankly, I found it incredibly naïve and even a little insulting. More importantly, though, it motivated me to get on the stick and write a book about a subject that's been on my mind for years now. Cooking for yourself doesn't need to feel like a chore or, perhaps worse, it doesn't need to bring to mind that character in Hitchcock's *Rear Window*. Remember Miss Lonely Hearts? As Jimmy Stewart's character watched through his binoculars from across the courtyard, she set a table for two, raised a glass, forced a smile, and mimed a romantic dinner with an empty chair.

Naturally, I'd love to share my life with someone. And I spend a not-insignificant amount of emotional energy looking for and nurturing the possibility of good relationships. But until the right one comes along, I gotta eat, I gotta cook, and I'm determined to do both well. When I make myself dinner, I don't pretend my true love is sitting across from me—I'm often too excited about the flavors I've just put together to think about much of anything else.

Serve Yourself is a celebration of this dynamic, and I hope it becomes an indispensable guide for all those food-loving single cooks who need ideas to help them face some of the most common challenges: How do you feed yourself well without continually resorting to recipes that serve four or six or more, leaving you with leftovers for days or, God forbid, weeks? Some meals are worth eating more than once, but we solo artists deserve just as varied a diet as anyone. While I love having some leftovers around that can morph into new dishes, I also appreciate the beauty of starting and finishing a single cooking project on a given night. If I want more, it's much easier to double a recipe that's written for one than it is to shrink one for six.

Believe it or not, these strategies aren't just for singles, either. Most modern couples I know consist of at least one person who frequently works past the dinner hour or is out of town for days at a time on business. To paraphrase Cher (I've always wanted to write that), sooner or later, we all eat alone.

There's enough of us solo dwellers—more than 31 million in the United States alone—that you'd think there would've been scores of cookbooks on the subject by now. Single-person households have been the fastest-growing census category in America since the 1980s, making up more than a quarter of all homes, and the category is continuing to grow. Young people are waiting longer to get married, or are foregoing it altogether, while older people who outlive their spouses are healthy enough to live independently.

My own lessons in independent living and cooking began when I was a kid, thanks to my mom and stepdad, Vern. My mother let me use her stand mixer to whip the cream or potatoes, and Vern taught me to make chicken-fried steak and cornmeal-coated pan-fried catfish. Perhaps most importantly, I started grocery shopping for the family at age eight.

The latter happened after my parents' divorce, once my mother realized that although she had lost privileges to shop at the commissary, the steeply discounted grocery store on Goodfellow Air Force Base for military personnel and their dependents, her kids had not. So she made up a list, handed me cash, and drove me to the store. The first time she worried: "Are you all right doing this, honey? I'll be right out here if you need me."

When an hour later, the store worker who bagged our groceries followed me outside to the car, he initially didn't see my mother waiting for me. As she loves to tell it, he took one look at the car and said, "Don't tell me you can drive, too."

My mother wasn't worried about me for long, because my enthusiasm was so obvious. And why wouldn't it be? I was like a kid in a candy store—okay, a grocery store—and I felt liberated. I followed her list to the letter, but I had to make choices among brands, look for cheaper substitutions, and remember the all-important goal: If I finished under budget, I could pick out something just for myself.

It was the first of many little things that helped me feel comfortable many years later when I moved to a new city and an apartment all my own, especially once I learned how to shop and cook for just one rather than a family of four.

The thing to remember is this: You don't have to resort to takeout just because you live alone. You can keep the right (delicious) foods in your pantry, refrigerator, and freezer; learn to shop with an eye for ingredients that support a single cook's lifestyle; and cook without worrying about satisfying anyone's hankerings but your own.

After all, if you don't feed yourself well, who will?

ACKNOWLEDGMENTS

A writer doesn't work alone, even on a cookbook about cooking alone. I've had more help than I can probably even remember, or certainly keep track of, so my apologies for any omissions in this list.

That said, plenty of people rise to the top of those who deserve thanks. First of all, this book never would have happened if *Washington Post* deputy food editor Bonnie Benwick hadn't suggested that cooking for one, a topic we covered in a few feature stories, deserved a monthly column, and then indulged me later when I claimed the topic all for myself. As my editor on the column, she has been an invaluable sounding board and reality check, brainstorming approaches, displaying admirable patience, and asking just the right questions. She encouraged the writing of this book, gave honest and helpful feedback on my cooking and recipes, and helped test recipes.

My sister, Rebekah, is truly awe-inspiring in many ways, but in recent years she has shown me how possible it is to become so close to the source of your food that the line between you and it is practically nonexistent.

My sources for the monthly column—fellow cooks, bloggers, and authors—gave freely of their time, expertise, and recipes, and they responded to my questions, however silly. The first among these is the incomparable Judith Jones, whose book, *The Pleasures of Cooking for One*, is an icon of this growing genre. Also Eric Ripert, Joyce Goldstein, Deborah Madison, Suzanne Pirret, Debby Maugans Nakos, Jim Lahey, Steve Sando, Lidia Bastianich, Jaden Hair, K. N. Vinod, Harumi Kurihara, Russell Warnick, Michele Humes, Grace Young, and Lynn Alley.

My agent, Lisa Ekus, and her daughter and associate, Sally Ekus, are always quick with words of support and practical advice. I'm proud that the sale of my book was Sally's first.

My editor at Ten Speed Press, Dawn Yanagihara, stood at the ready to play devil's advocate just when I needed to hear it and handled my work with efficient grace. I knew her from her Boston days and couldn't have asked for a better match. Copy editor Andrea Chesman nipped and tucked, tweaked and massaged my copy until it shone. When Dawn moved on from Ten Speed after my book was through the copy-editor phase, Jenny Wapner picked up where she left off and shepherded the project to completion with the same helpful attitude and can-do spirit.

I was thrilled when I learned that Ed Anderson, whose work I have admired for years, would shoot the photographs for this book; the thrill continued every time I saw another image. He and food stylist Jenny Martin-Wong made the dishes look effortless, which is exactly right.

Heidi Robb is a recipe wizard, and she lent me use of her creative mind and unerring palate as she performed triage on several dishes that were giving me trouble, helping me turn them into winners.

Several friends and colleagues tasted my cooking and provided the most important things possible to a cookbook author: open minds, expert palates, and honest feedback. These include Jane Black, Becky Krystal, Zofia Smardz, David Hagedorn, Michael Widomski, Sean Finnell, Jamie Bennett, Jon Kelly, and Yaron Peleg.

Testing was cheerfully and ably handled by students and alumni of Cambridge School of Culinary Arts, coordinated by Elizabeth Dayton. When midterms approached, friends, family, and colleagues took up the reins: Carol Blymire, Robin Shuster, Necee Regis, Jane Touzalin, Josh Bloom, Rebekah Yonan, Gary Bowden, Mark Ziomek, Brent Cunningham, Devra First, Harry and Eve First, Kim Watson, Christy Goldfinch, Lydia Walshin, Edouard Fontenot, Jerry Sealy, Rachel Alabiso, Wayne Winters, Alex Knight, Doug Campbell, Ted Weesner, Michael Coccola, and Ari Shapiro.

Several friends and fellow cooks/authors came through with support and guidance—and fantastic recipes. At the top of this list is Patricia Jinich, my go-to source for all questions about Mexican cuisine. Domenica Marchetti and Samuel Fromartz came through with a pasta dish and a pizza dough, respectively, and I'm grateful. The inimitable Lidia Bastianich, queen of family-style cooking, responded to my plea with some unerringly smart ideas.

Some people have encouraged this book from its earliest inception and have offered welcome advice and perspective: Susan Puckett, Bill Addison, Kim O'Donnel, Monica Bhide, Kathleen Finn, Tim Carman, Raju Narisetti, Tom Sietsema, and Nancy Wall Hopkins. Others have been inspirations without, perhaps, knowing it: Peter Reinhart, David Lebovitz, Rose Levy Beranbaum, Karen Page and Andrew Dornenburg, Michael Ruhlman, Dorie Greenspan, Diana Kennedy, Anya von Bremzen, Giuliano Hazan, Marcella Hazan, and Ed Levine.

I sometimes think my brothers and sisters could star in a TV cooking reality show in which we each represent a stereotypical cook: the busy suburban mom (Julie), the small-town Texas barbecue fanatic (Michael), the genteel Southern lady (Teri), the down-home queen of pies (Nancy), and the back-to-the-land-er (Rebekah). They all inspired me in their own ways, as did my late sister, Bonnie, and father, Richard. My mom deserves credit for getting me interested in food before I was interested in almost anything else, and I'm already on record as crediting my stepdad, Vern, with teaching me how to make my first real dish, chicken-fried steak.

CHAPTER 1
BASIC RECIPES, CONDIMENTS, AND PICKLES

· ·

When editors of Washington D.C.'s Brightest Young Things blog emailed and asked if they could catalog and photograph everything in my fridge and freezer for a series they were working on, I had one immediate question: "How much time do you have?"

The answer was, "As much time as we need," which was good, because it took more than two hours, and that was working as quickly as we could. My entry must've had at least twice the items of any of the other foodniks featured in the series. Friends who posted the link on Facebook said things like, "I have fridge-envy," and they weren't talking about the appliance.

As a single cook, why do I have so much food? Well, before you accuse me of hoarding, let me get on my soap box: I'm a zealot about the fact that if you're fully stocked, making something quick at the end of a long workday is that much easier. I think it might even be more important for single folks than for others, because it allows us to make bigger batches of things when we have the time, but then just use a little of it to help punch up a single-serving meal that doesn't result in a mountain of leftovers.

I certainly have more than my fair share of store-bought condiments, but I also like to make my own. I know just what's in them (no unpronounceable ingredients here), I can make them to suit my own sometimes-quirky palate, and I positively savor the satisfaction—or should I say self-satisfaction?—when I use them.

12-HOUR TOMATOES

Makes about 3 cups

· ·

I have made these tomatoes for more than a decade now, but it wasn't until my sister's homegrown Maine wedding, where I made hundreds of them for the appetizer table, that I realized how perfect a technique this is for "putting up" local tomatoes in the peak season. The low heat of the oven turns the tomatoes almost jammy, concentrating the flavor beautifully, which makes them perfect as a topping for bruschetta, pasta, or pizza (see Smoky Pizza Margherita, page 106). They also can be served on an antipasti platter with mixed olives, cheese, pickles, and/or smoked fish. I call them 12-hour tomatoes, but the amount of time it takes depends greatly on the size and juiciness of the tomatoes. So for the least fuss, don't mix varieties or sizes in one batch, but feel free to multiply this recipe as you wish. Left in the oven long enough, the tomatoes will start to become a little chewy around the edges, which make a nice counterpoint to the moisture inside. Try other spices instead of the cumin: regular paprika, smoked Spanish paprika (pimenton), and cinnamon also work well with the tomatoes, or you can stick with just salt and pepper for the purest tomato flavor.

· ·

4 teaspoons cumin seeds
8 large (3- to 4-inch) tomatoes, stemmed (but not cored) and cut in half vertically

Kosher or sea salt
Freshly ground black pepper
¼ cup extra-virgin olive oil, plus more for storing

Preheat the oven to 200°F. Line a large rimmed baking sheet with aluminum foil or parchment paper.

Place a small, dry skillet over medium heat. Add the seeds and toast, shaking the pan occasionally, until they are fragrant but not browned, 2 to 4 minutes. Immediately transfer them to a heatproof bowl to stop the cooking; let cool completely, and then grind.

Place the tomatoes, cut side up, on the prepared baking sheet. Season the cut side with salt and pepper to taste, then drizzle with oil. Sprinkle evenly with the ground cumin.

Bake for 10 to 14 hours (the time will vary, depending on the size and variety of tomato), until the tomatoes have collapsed and shriveled to ¼ to ½ inch thick; they should still be moist inside but can be slightly crisp and browned at the edges.

Cool completely. To store, pack the tomatoes in an airtight container, cover them with olive oil, and refrigerate for up to 2 weeks. For longer storage, use a thermometer to make sure your refrigerator is under 38°F, then pack them tightly into sterilized jars, cover them with olive oil, and refrigerate for up to 3 months. Or pack them into freezer-safe plastic bags, remove as much air as possible from the bags, and freeze for up to 6 months. Defrost an entire bag at a time; once defrosted, cover tomatoes with olive oil and store in the fridge.

CORN BROTH

Makes 4 to 5 cups

. . . .

It's too bad so many cooks, when presented with a basket of beautifully fresh and local corn, strip off those husks and toss them. That's a lot of flavor headed for the compost pile or, worse, the trash. I got the idea to use the husks to make corn broth from Vitaly Paley of Paley's Place in Portland, Oregon, as mentioned in *The Flavor Bible* by Karen Page and Andrew Dornenburg. I was already using the cobs, so I threw the husks in the pot along with the silks, too, to get as much corn flavor as possible. This broth is best made in the very height of local corn season and won't be as vibrant with supermarket corn. Once you have the broth on hand, use it as the base for soups, especially as a stand-in for chicken broth in Corn Risotto with Roasted Cherry Tomatoes (page 135) and add it in increments to sauces for a boost of summer flavor.

. . . .

4 whole ears corn
7 cups water

Rinse the corn, then strip off the husks and silks. Discard any browned or blackened spots of silk and coarsely cut the remaining husks and silks into 2- to 3-inch pieces. Use a vegetable brush and running water to remove any remaining silks from the ears.

Remove the kernels by cutting each cob in half, and then standing it on its flat end on a cutting board. Use a knife to slice the kernels off from top to bottom. Reserve the kernels for another use (freezing them if necessary). Cut the stripped cobs into 2- to 3-inch pieces and transfer them to a large stockpot. Cover with the husks and silks.

Add the water and place the pot over medium-high heat. Bring to a boil, then reduce the heat to low to keep the liquid at a bare simmer; cover and cook undisturbed until very fragrant, about 1 hour.

Strain the broth through a fine-mesh strainer into a large bowl, pressing on the solids to extract as much liquid as possible. Discard the husks, cobs, and silks. Strain again if needed to remove any remaining silks. The broth can be used right away; or let it cool to room temperature, then portion it into heavy-duty resealable plastic food storage bags or ice cube trays. Refrigerate for up to 3 days or freeze for up to 2 months.

HERBED LEMON CONFIT

Makes about 2 cups

Preserved lemons can spike up the flavor of any dish, particularly something rich that needs the cut-through-the-fat talents only an acidic ingredient can bring. This method, which I based on a recipe in Tom Colicchio's *'wichcraft* (Clarkson Potter, 2009), drastically reduces the amount of time it takes to preserve lemons by slicing them first, allowing the salt/sugar mixture to penetrate that much more quickly. And that's a good thing, because you won't want to wait too long for these. They need 3 days of curing time, but they will keep in an airtight container in your refrigerator for a month. Use them in Smoked Trout, Potato, and Fennel Pizza (page 113); Roast Chicken Leg with Gremolata and Sunchokes (page 72); and Tuna, Chickpea, and Arugula Sandwich (page 126); or anywhere else you want a sharp hit of salty lemon.

3 lemons
1 large shallot lobe, finely chopped
2 cloves garlic, finely chopped
Leaves from 1 large sprig rosemary, finely chopped
Leaves from 1 sprig thyme

6 black peppercorns, crushed
3 tablespoons coarse kosher or sea salt
1 tablespoon sugar
½ to 1 cup extra-virgin olive oil

Bring a medium pot of water to a boil over high heat, then plunge the lemons into the water for about 30 seconds or so, to soften any wax on the fruit. Drain, rinse, wipe the lemons clean, and dry them. Cut the lemons into very thin slices, discarding the ends and any seeds.

Combine the shallot, garlic, rosemary, thyme, and peppercorns in a small bowl. Combine the salt and sugar in a separate small bowl.

Arrange a layer of lemon slices in the bottom of a medium container with a lid, being sure not to overlap the slices. Sprinkle the lemons first with a little of the shallot-garlic mixture, then with some of the salt-sugar mixture. Repeat to use all the slices, layering them in several stacks and sprinkling them alternately with the two mixtures until the final lemon slices are topped with the last of the shallot-garlic and salt-sugar mixtures. Cover tightly and refrigerate for 3 days, but after a day or so, turn over the container so all the slices can cure evenly.

Drain the lemons in a strainer for about 15 minutes. Have ready a clean 1-quart container with a tight-fitting lid.

Pack the drained lemons tightly in the container, then fill with the oil, making sure the lemons are completely covered. The confit can be used immediately or refrigerated for up to 1 month.

SPICY HUMMUS

Makes about 2 cups

. . . .

I love hummus, but ever since I had the justifiably famous spicy version at Sahadi's, a Middle Eastern specialty foods shop in Brooklyn, I'm not satisfied with the tame stuff anymore. This is not their recipe, but it wasn't hard to add a little fire to my favorite one, which uses more water than you might think, resulting in a particularly silky hummus. Eat some immediately, of course, with crackers or bread or whatever suits your fancy, but make sure to save some for Eggplant and Spicy Hummus Flatbread (page 111), and refrigerate the rest for up to 2 weeks, during which time you can use it as a sandwich spread or even thin it out with vinegar to make a salad dressing. A shortcut, obviously, is to add the pepper-infused olive oil to your favorite store-bought hummus.

. . . .

1 tablespoon extra-virgin olive oil
1 teaspoon red pepper flakes
½ teaspoon pimenton (smoked Spanish paprika)
2 cups cooked chickpeas, preferably homemade (page 45), rinsed and drained
½ cup chickpea cooking liquid or water, plus more as needed

2 tablespoons tahini, plus more as needed
Juice of 1 lemon
1 plump clove garlic, peeled
½ teaspoon salt, plus more to taste

Pour the oil into a small skillet over medium heat. When the oil starts to shimmer, sprinkle in the red pepper flakes and pimenton. Cook, stirring or shaking the pan frequently, until the spices are very fragrant, about 30 seconds. (Be careful not to let the spices burn.) Turn off the heat and let cool.

In a food processor, combine the chickpeas, cooking liquid, tahini, lemon juice, garlic, and salt. Pour in the oil and red pepper flakes from the skillet. Process until smooth. Taste, adjust the salt if necessary, and add more cooking liquid or water if you want the hummus thinner or more tahini if you want it thicker.

Eat immediately, or cover tightly and store in the refrigerator for up to 2 weeks.

MULLED WINE SYRUP

Makes ½ cup

I used to be reluctant to open a bottle of wine at home unless I was entertaining, because I'd drink a glass or two and then have to contend with the leftover vino. There are various ways to deal with it (see sidebar, page 23), but once I discovered this idea from blogger Michele Humes on SeriousEats.com, it was a problem no more. Even lesser-quality wine becomes a deeply flavored condiment good for drizzling on ice cream, chocolate desserts, or citrus segments. It can be used for layering in a parfait with Greek-style yogurt (see page 161) or for hydrating dried cherries in a tart with almonds (page 163). I tend to use whatever spices strike my fancy at the time; with red wine, I like this particular combination, but whole cinnamon, cloves, and/or allspice, for example, could be used for a more pronounced flavor. The best thing about this syrup? Once you cool it, it can be refrigerated in an airtight container indefinitely.

1½ cups red wine of any variety
½ cup sugar
1 vanilla bean, split (not scraped)

2 whole star anise
1 teaspoon pink peppercorns

Combine the wine, sugar, vanilla bean, star anise, and peppercorns in a wide pot or skillet over medium-high heat, stirring to dissolve the sugar. Bring to a boil, then decrease the heat to medium; cook until the liquid becomes syrupy and has reduced by about two-thirds, about 10 minutes.

Use a fine-mesh strainer to strain the syrup into a small container; discard the spices and let cool. Use immediately or cover and refrigerate.

Variation: Use white wine instead of red, and use 1 vanilla bean and five or six ¼-inch slices of fresh ginger.

CASHEW TAMARI DRESSING

Makes about 1½ cups

· ·

While I was in college (along with 49,999 of my closest friends at the University of Texas at Austin), I was one of the many nonvegetarian fans of Mother's, an iconic vegetarian restaurant in Hyde Park, where I'd pretty much always get a smoothie and a huge spinach salad with this pungent dressing. Besides cashews, the main ingredient is tamari, a richer version of soy sauce that's traditionally (but not always) made without wheat. Decades later, Mother's is still going strong, reopening after a 2007 fire and still serving this dressing (bottling it for retail sale, even). Thanks to the glories of Google, I was able to track down a recipe for it from Rachel MacIntyre, a personal chef in Austin who blogs at thefriendlykitchen.com and used to work at Mother's precursor, West Lynn Cafe. I lightened it a little bit, but it's as addictive as ever. I toss it onto spinach and other salads, of course, but also baked potatoes, broiled asparagus, steamed carrots, and more, including Charred Asparagus, Tofu, and Farro Salad (page 144).

· ·

½ cup extra-virgin olive oil
2 tablespoons balsamic vinegar
6 tablespoons tamari

½ cup raw, unsalted cashews
¼ cup water

In a blender or food processor, combine the oil, vinegar, tamari, cashews, and water. Pulse several times until the mixture is emulsified but there are still bits of cashew throughout. Taste for flavors and adjust as needed. Store in an airtight container in the refrigerator for several weeks.

Note: The dressing will congeal in the refrigerator, so let it come to room temperature before using, or zap it in the microwave for a few seconds to speed things up.

PARSLEY GARLIC DRESSING

Makes about 2 cups

. . . .

When I lived in Peterborough, New Hampshire, in the early 1990s, I had two obsessions. The first was the lettuce mix from organic farming pioneer Rosaly Bass, who charmed me so much I signed up for a subscription that let me pick what I wanted off her land all season long. (I tended to swing by at midnight after a long day as editor of the weekly *Monadnock Ledger* and shovel up carrots by moonlight.) The second was this powerfully sharp dressing, made by chef Hiroshi Hayashi at his elegant, health-minded Japanese restaurant, Latacarta. While Rosaly's farm is still going strong, Hayashi long ago closed the restaurant and started the Monadnock School of Natural Cooking and Philosophy, but he still makes this vegan dressing. I use it to dress simple salads of butter lettuce with cherry tomatoes and carrots, taking care to slice the carrots into a perfect julienne the way I remember Hayashi did. The dressing also makes an excellent dip for crudités.

. . . .

1 (12-ounce) block silken tofu, drained
1 large or 2 small cloves garlic
¼ large bunch parsley (about 1 cup coarsely
   chopped leaves and stems)
Juice of 1 lemon

¼ cup unseasond rice vinegar
¼ cup extra-virgin olive oil
1 teaspoon coarse kosher or sea salt
¼ teaspoon cayenne pepper

Combine all the ingredients in a blender or food processor and blend until smooth. Use immediately, or refrigerate for up to 2 weeks.

CILANTRO VINAIGRETTE

Makes about ¾ cup

I got this recipe from Patricia Jinich, chef-instructor at the Mexican Cultural Institute in Washington, D.C., who got it from her sister. Don't be fooled by its simplicity; it is perfectly balanced. It will keep its lively color for about a week in the refrigerator, but the flavor will last another week or two, meaning you can feel free to splash it onto all manner of salads, plus avocados, tomatoes, green beans, even cold rice. You can also use other leafy herbs, particularly parsley, basil, or mint, instead of the cilantro.

¼ cup fresh cilantro leaves, coarsely chopped
¼ cup extra-virgin olive oil
¼ cup canola oil
¼ cup red wine vinegar

1 clove garlic, coarsely chopped
1 teaspoon sugar
½ teaspoon salt

Combine all the ingredients in a blender, cover, and puree until smooth. Use immediately, or refrigerate for up to 3 weeks.

BLUEBERRY LEMON JAM

Makes 4 half-pint jars

This recipe started the way all jam recipes should: I came into a bounty of stunningly delicious, in-season fruit. It wasn't from a blueberry patch like those in southern Maine my homesteading sister, Rebekah, picks from, but it was the closest thing I have to such: the Dupont Circle FreshFarm Market. One of my favorite vendors there, Tree and Leaf, had blueberries one summer that were better than any I've tasted outside Maine. I paid a pretty penny for them, went home, and broke open *Mes Confitures*, the tome by famous French jam maker Christine Ferber. I found her take on a wild blueberry–lemon jam, and I took shameless liberties with it, as anybody working with much different fruit should. I used much less sugar (her wild ones must be very tart), and streamlined the process. The result is a celebration of the blueberry, brightened with slices of candied lemon, peel and all. Use it anytime you want good jam: on toast, stirred into yogurt, and even as the basis of such desserts as Blueberry-Lemon Tart with Toasted Coconut (page 165).

2 lemons, thinly sliced and seeded
⅓ cup water

1¼ cups sugar
2 pounds blueberries, stemmed

Have ready four 8-ounce canning jars with 2-piece lids. Fill a large pot with water and bring to a boil over high heat, then decrease the heat so that the water is barely bubbling. Immerse the pint jars in the canning kettle. Place the rings and lids in a separate small saucepan and cover them with hot water. Leave the jars and lids immersed while you cook the jam. If you don't have a candy thermometer to tell you when the jam is done, place a small plate in the freezer.

Combine the lemon slices, water, and ½ cup of the sugar in a large saucepan over medium-high heat; bring to a boil and cook undisturbed until the lemon slices are translucent, about 20 minutes. Add the remaining ¾ cup sugar and the blueberries; cook, stirring occasionally, until the mixture thickens and reaches 220°F on a candy thermometer, 20 to 30 minutes.

If you don't have a candy thermometer, remove the plate from the freezer and immediately spoon a teaspoon of jam onto it. Let it sit for a few minutes until the jam cools, then tilt the plate and see how much it runs. It will probably not wrinkle and get firm the way jams with more pectin would, but it should be thick and only slightly run. If it's too runny, continue cooking it down, stirring frequently, until it thickens further.

While the jam is still hot, ladle it into the hot, sterilized canning jars, leaving about ¼ inch of head space at the top. Remove any air bubbles by running a long, nonmetallic utensil, such as a chopstick or wooden skewer, between the jar and the jam. Top with the prepared lids, close tightly, and process for 5 minutes in a hot-water bath with the jars submerged by at least 1 to 2 inches of water. Remove from the water and let cool, undisturbed, to room temperature.

Besides making that telltale ping when it seals, the lid of a properly sealed jar should be slightly concave and not move; if the lid springs down and back when you press your finger in the center, the lid is unsealed. If it doesn't seal, process it again or store it in the refrigerator instead of at room temperature. Store sealed jars in a cool, dry place.

Note: If you don't want to fully seal and can the jam, you can pack it into clean jars, tighten the lids, let cool to room temperature, and refrigerate for several months. Or pack into freezer-safe plastic bags, squeeze out the extra air, seal, and freeze for up to one year.

STRAWBERRY VANILLA JAM

Makes 8 half-pint jars

. . . .

When I spent a day making jams with Stefano Frigerio, a chef-turned-food-producer, I knew I had found a kindred spirit. Frigerio, who sells his Copper Pot Food Co. jams, sauces, and pastas at Washington, D.C., farmers' markets, resisted set-in-stone recipes and instead cautioned me that the most important thing is to taste, especially if you don't want the jam to be too sweet. In the true spirit of preserving, use only fresh, local, in-season berries for this jam. (There's really no reason to preserve something that you can get all year-round, so why use supermarket strawberries?) Without any added pectin, this jam has a slightly loose consistency, which I like, given that my favorite use is to stir it into yogurt.

. . . .

6 quarts (about 8 pounds) strawberries, hulled and halved

6 vanilla beans, slit lengthwise with a sharp knife
1½ to 2 cups sugar, plus more to taste

Combine the strawberries, vanilla beans, and 1½ cups of the sugar in a large bowl. Mix well and let the mixture sit for at least 30 minutes, or until a puddle of juice forms at the bottom of the bowl, and up to several hours.

Meanwhile, have ready 8 half-pint canning jars with 2-piece lids. Fill a large pot with water and bring to a boil over high heat, then reduce the heat so that the water is barely bubbling. Immerse the pint jars in the pot. Place the rings and lids in a separate small saucepan and cover them with very hot, but not boiling, water. Leave the jars and lids immersed while you cook the jam. If you don't have a candy thermometer to tell you when the jam is done, place a small plate in the freezer.

Transfer the fruit mixture and all of its juices to a large, wide pot set over medium-high heat. Cook, stirring occasionally, until the strawberries are very

soft, 25 to 30 minutes. Use a potato masher to break down the strawberries. Taste, and add additional sugar, ¼ cup at a time, stirring to dissolve it, as needed. Fish out the vanilla beans and use a paring knife to scrape their seeds into the jam. Discard the beans.

Continue cooking the mixture, stirring frequently to avoid scorching, until it reduces by about one-third and reaches 220°F on a candy thermometer, another 60 to 90 minutes. If you don't have a candy thermometer, remove the plate from the freezer and immediately spoon a teaspoon of jam onto it. Let it sit for a few minutes until the jam cools, then tilt the plate and see how much it runs. It will probably not wrinkle and get firm the way jams with more pectin would, but it should be thick and only slightly run. If it's too runny, continue cooking it down, stirring frequently, until it thickens further.

While the jam is still hot, ladle it into the hot, sterilized canning jars, leaving about ¼ inch of head space at the top. Remove any air bubbles by running a long, nonmetallic utensil, such as a chopstick or wooden skewer, around the edges of the jar between the jar and the jam. Top with the prepared lids, close tightly, and process for 5 minutes in a hot-water bath (submerge the jars by at least 1 to 2 inches of water). Let cool, undisturbed, to room temperature.

Besides making that telltale ping when it seals, the lid of a properly sealed jar should be slightly concave and not move when touched; if the lid springs down and back when you press your finger in the center, the lid is not sealed. Process it again, or store the jar in the refrigerator instead of at room temperature. Store jars in a cool, dry place.

Note: If you don't want to fully seal and can the jam, you can pack it into clean jars, tighten the lids, let cool to room temperature, and refrigerate for several months. Or pack into freezer-safe plastic bags, squeeze out the extra air, seal, and freeze for up to one year.

SALSA VERDE

Makes about 2 cups

· ·

Some people say that Tex-Mex cooking bears no relation to Mexican. Well, tell that to me and my friend Patricia Jinich, a Mexico City native who now teaches cooking classes through the Mexican Cultural Institute in Washington, D.C. Pati and I bonded over our mutual love of Mexican food, and even though I have traveled frequently in Mexico, many of the recipes she has shared with me take me right back to my West Texas childhood or Central Texas college days. This salsa—gorgeous to behold and tart and spicy to taste—is the perfect example; its flavors are identical to those served up in little bowls on every table at the best Tex-Mex restaurants I know. It's perfect on the Catfish Tacos with Chipotle Slaw (page 101) and Shrimp Tacos with Grapefruit–Black Bean Salsa (page 102), and it is a natural pairing with seafood. But, honestly, you can drizzle it on just about anything to decent effect. And, of course, you can just scoop it up with tortilla chips.

· ·

1 pound tomatillos, husks removed and rinsed
2 cloves garlic
2 jalapeño chiles, stems removed
Leaves from ½ bunch cilantro (about ½ cup packed)

1 large shallot lobe or small onion, chopped (about ¼ cup)
½ teaspoon coarse kosher or sea salt, plus more to taste
1 tablespoon vegetable oil

Combine the tomatillos, garlic, and jalapeños in a medium pot and cover with water. Place over high heat and bring to a boil. Decrease the heat to medium and cook until the tomatillos change in color from bright to pale olive green and are quite soft but not yet coming apart, about 10 minutes.

Transfer the tomatillos, garlic, one of the jalapeños, and ½ cup of the cooking liquid to a blender; remove the center of the lid and place a dish towel over it so steam can escape. Puree until smooth. (If you have an immersion or handheld blender, you can do this right in the pot; pour out all but ½ cup of the cooking liquid and fish out one of the jalapeños before proceeding.)

Add the cilantro, shallot, and salt; puree until smooth. Taste and add salt as needed. Also taste for heat and add part or all of the remaining jalapeño, if desired, and puree.

Discard the cooking water in the pot, pour in the vegetable oil, and return the pot to medium-high heat. Add the sauce and bring to a boil, then decrease the heat to medium-low and simmer the sauce until it thickens a bit and deepens in flavor and color, about 5 minutes.

Transfer to a container to cool completely. Use immediately, or refrigerate for up to several weeks.

Clockwise from top left: Salsa Verde (page 14), Herbed Lemon Confit (page 4), Citrus Pickled Onions (page 19), and 12-Hour Tomatoes (page 2).

BLACKENED SALSA

Makes ¾ to 1 cup

My friend Karin and I moved to Boston at about the same time, and of all the things this fellow Tex-pat and I missed the most, at the top of the list was the spicy, smoky, black-flecked salsa at La Fogata restaurant in San Antonio, where Karin grew up and where we both loved to visit when we were in college in nearby Austin. In those days, La Fogata would sell you the stuff to go, but only if you brought your own container. Karin would fly back to Boston with a gallon jug in her carry-on, something that wouldn't go over too well with the TSA anymore. Nowadays, you can order the salsa online, but it's not quite the same, no doubt due to the preservatives required to make it shelf stable. After I saw a take on the recipe at SpiceLines.com, I started experimenting and developed my own. In addition to gracing the top of Tacos de Huevos (page 87) and going into Spicy Glazed Mini Meatloaf (page 65), the pungent, garlicky condiment is good on grilled pork chops or steak. Of course, it can be served as an appetizer with tortilla chips. The recipe doubles and triples easily.

1 jalapeño chile, stemmed and left whole
2 medium shallot lobes, peeled but left whole
4 cloves garlic, unpeeled
1 pint cherry tomatoes, stems removed

2 teaspoons sherry vinegar or red wine vinegar
½ teaspoon coarse kosher or sea salt, plus more as needed
¼ cup water, plus more as needed

Preheat the broiler with the rack set 3 to 4 inches from the element or flame.

Combine the jalapeño, shallots, garlic, and cherry tomatoes in a large cast-iron skillet or a roasting pan. Broil for 10 to 15 minutes, shaking the pan occasionally, until the vegetables are blackened all over.

Remove from the broiler and reserve the garlic and jalapeño; transfer the remaining vegetables to a food processor and let cool slightly.

When the garlic is cool enough to handle, discard the papery skin; add the garlic to the food processor. Slice open the jalapeño; scrape out the seeds and reserve them. Add the jalapeño to the food processor, along with the vinegar, salt, and water. Pulse or process briefly until the mixture is pureed but with some chunks remaining.

Taste and adjust salt as necessary; thin with water as needed. Adjust the heat level by adding as many of the reserved jalapeño seeds as desired, pulsing to combine. Serve immediately or refrigerate in an airtight container for up to 2 weeks.

RED PEPPER CHUTNEY

Makes about 2 cups

I'm a freak for sweet-and-sour flavors and an admitted chile-head. That's why I like Southeast Asian food so much, but the same combination of flavors characterizes food from other places, such as this rustic Italian-inspired chutney. I first made it when I was looking for single-serving appetizers: something small to calm my raging appetite (what I like to call "hanger") while I'm cooking. This flavor-packed condiment does the trick, particularly when served on top of good ricotta on toast. But it can also be one of those condiments that you keep around as the basis for main courses. Toss it in hot pasta, slather it on Three-Pepper Pizza with Goat Cheese (page 118), or use it to top Low, Slow, and Custardy Eggs (page 30) or Shrimp and Potato Chip Tortilla (page 36). I got the idea from the fabulous *A16: Food + Wine*, by Nate Appleman and Shelley Lindgren, but kicked it up by adding a poblano pepper, plus more red pepper flakes and garlic, and balanced it out with a little sugar.

2 large or 3 medium red bell peppers (about 1 pound total)
1 poblano pepper
2 tablespoons extra-virgin olive oil
1 tablespoon capers, drained
2 teaspoons tomato paste
3 large shallot lobes, cut into ¼-inch dice (about ½ cup)

1 clove garlic, chopped
¼ fennel bulb, cored and cut into ¼-inch dice (about ¼ cup)
½ teaspoon red pepper flakes
Kosher or sea salt
1 tablespoon red wine vinegar, plus more as needed
1 teaspoon sugar, plus more as needed

Preheat the broiler with the rack set 4 to 5 inches from the element or flame. Line a large baking sheet with aluminum foil.

Split the bell peppers and poblano pepper through the stems and lay them cut sides down on the prepared baking sheet. Broil for a few minutes, then turn the sheet front to back and broil for a few more minutes, until the peppers are completely charred. Remove from the broiler, and let them cool on the baking sheet. When the peppers are cool enough to handle, slip off and discard the peels, stems, cores, and seeds. (Resist the temptation to do any of this under running water, or the flavor will be lost.) Tear or cut the peppers into roughly equal strips about ½ inch wide.

Heat the oil in a large skillet over medium heat. Use paper towels to pat dry the capers. Add them to the hot oil and fry until they bloom and start to become crisp, 2 to 4 minutes. Add the tomato paste (be careful of splatters) and cook, stirring, until it darkens in color, about 2 minutes. Add the shallots, garlic, fennel, red pepper flakes, and salt to taste. Cook, stirring occasionally, until the vegetables are tender, about 5 minutes.

Add the vinegar and use a spatula to dislodge any browned bits from the bottom of the skillet, then stir in the sugar. Add the peppers and cook for a few minutes, stirring. Taste for seasoning, adding salt, vinegar, or sugar as needed.

Serve the chutney warm or at room temperature. Or let it cool, then refrigerate in a tightly covered container for up to 2 weeks.

CABBAGE AND PEAR KIMCHI

Makes about 4 cups

Like many food-oriented folk, I have a serious kimchi obsession going. But I didn't want just any old kimchi recipe in this book. And I knew just where to turn in search of a recipe that has a little something extra: my friend Deb Samuels, cooking teacher and coauthor with Taekyung Chung of *The Korean Table: From Barbecue to Bibimbap*. Deb keeps up on all things Korean, and she told me that not only is it becoming more fashionable to salt kimchi less than traditional recipes call for, but also that the water-soaking process probably can be skipped entirely. She also said one of her favorites is a white kimchi with a main ingredient of Asian pear, which happened to already feature strongly in my Korean Short Rib Tacos (page 92). Why not try a kimchi with cabbage and pear together? Of course, she was right on the money. Look for Korean chili powder, which has a distinctive heat but a mellow, sweet undertone, in Asian supermarkets; for kimchi, there really is no substitute. Once you have your ingredients, this kimchi could hardly be simpler to make, and the slight sweetness and crunch it gets from the pear make it positively haunting. Besides using it on the tacos, use it on Kimchi, Ham, and Fried Egg Pizza (page 107) and Fried Rice with Cauliflower and Kimchi (page 136).

1 head napa cabbage (1½ to 2 pounds), cored and
    cut into 2-inch pieces
1 tablespoon coarse kosher or sea salt
1 Asian pear, cored and cut into ½-inch dice
    (do not peel)
¼ cup Korean red chili powder
6 cloves garlic, peeled

2-inch piece fresh ginger, peeled and coarsely
    chopped
2 tablespoons water
2 teaspoons sugar
2 teaspoons oyster sauce
2 teaspoons Asian fish sauce

Toss the cabbage with the salt in a large bowl. Let it sit until it exudes liquid and wilts, 60 to 90 minutes. Lift the cabbage out of the excess liquid by the handful, squeeze it dry, and transfer it to another bowl, discarding the liquid. Do not rinse.

Stir in the Asian pear, tossing to combine.

Combine the chili powder, garlic, ginger, water, sugar, oyster sauce, and fish sauce in a food processor. Process until smooth, scraping down the sides of the bowl if needed. Add to the cabbage-pear mixture, toss to combine, and let sit overnight, covered and at room temperature.

Transfer the mixture to an airtight container and refrigerate. Wait at least a few days before using the kimchi, which will get more pungent as the days go by. Use within 2 weeks.

CITRUS-PICKLED ONIONS

Makes about 2 cups

Pickled onions are the magic fix-it condiment in my refrigerator. You could serve me the worst dish ever, and if it had a few pickled onions on top, I'd probably say, "Hmm. Not bad." Of course, that means that they can also take something that's already delicious and make it spectacular. They're a traditional partner with pibils, the banana leaf–wrapped, pit-cooked meats of the Yucatan. I particularly like them on tacos (see Cochinita Pibil Tacos with Habanero Salsa, page 95, and Tacos de Huevos, page 87), where they give an extra crunch and hit of acidity. I've made them all sorts of ways over the years—combining the onions with lime juice, salt, and cumin; blanching the onions first, then tossing in vinegar and Tabasco—but it wasn't until my delightful friend Patricia Jinich turned me on to her method that I made it mine, too. Pati, who blogs at patismexicantable. com, experimented endlessly (well, sixteen batches) to find the right combination that would substitute for Yucatecan bitter orange juice before she settled on this one. It was worth it, but if you can find bitter orange (labeled *naranja agria* in Latin stores), use it instead of the juice/vinegar combination here.

1 banana chile or jalapeño chile
¼ cup freshly squeezed grapefruit juice
¼ cup freshly squeezed orange juice
¼ cup freshly squeezed lime juice
¼ cup distilled white vinegar
¼ teaspoon freshly ground black pepper

¼ teaspoon ground allspice
½ teaspoon coarse kosher or sea salt, or more to taste
1 large red onion, thinly sliced (about 2 cups)
2 bay leaves

Char the chile by holding it with tongs directly over the open flame of a gas burner, turning a few times, until the skin is lightly charred, 3 to 6 minutes. (If you don't have a gas stove, you can do this under the broiler.) Slash open the chile.

In a large mixing bowl, combine the citrus juices with the vinegar, black pepper, allspice, and salt, and mix well. Add the red onion slices, bay leaves, and chile and toss to combine.

Let the mixture sit at room temperature for at least 2 hours and up to 6 hours. Transfer to a large glass jar, cover tightly, and store in the refrigerator for up to 2 weeks.

PICKLED ANCHOS

Makes about ¾ cup

• •

Why didn't I think of these? I've long been in love with pickled (fresh) jalapeños, and I've certainly spent enough time hydrating dried chile peppers. This recipe, from chef David Suarez of Rosa Mexicano restaurant in Washington, D.C., combines both ideas in one. They're simple to make and last for up to 2 weeks in the refrigerator. You'll want to pull them out for anything that needs a sharp and spicy touch: tacos and nachos, of course, but also on Three-Pepper Pizza with Goat Cheese (page 118). Ancho chiles are easy to find, but if you have access to a wider selection of chile peppers, try this recipe with moritas, which have a unique fruity complexity.

• •

2 cups apple cider vinegar
2¾ cups sugar

3 ounces dried ancho chiles, stemmed, seeded, and cut or torn into 1-inch strips

Combine the vinegar and sugar in a small saucepan. Bring to a boil over high heat, stirring until the sugar has dissolved. Remove from the heat.

Add the ancho strips, making sure they are submerged. Let them sit for at least 1 hour, or until the anchos have softened. Drain them and use right away, or cover and refrigerate.

Note: After draining the anchos for use or storage, save the pickling liquid and splash it on salads with an equal amount of extra-virgin olive oil.

STORING AND USING EXTRA INGREDIENTS

One of the most vexing consequences of cooking for one is that sometimes, no matter how hard your trusty recipe writer tries, he can't avoid leftover ingredients. That means you may come away from the recipe with, say, half an avocado or three-quarters of a can of diced tomatoes. It's not a problem with something like dried beans, which store easily, but it can be for something perishable. I make up for leftovers in most cases by calling for those ingredients in other recipes. Here's a cheat sheet to help you find other ways to use up those leftover ingredients.

FRESH HERBS

If you can't grow them yourself, try to buy them from a farmers' market, because they'll last longer than store-bought. Store basil, mint, and parsley by treating them like cut flowers: Strip off the bottom leaves, cut the stems at a diagonal, and place in a glass of fresh water on your countertop, changing the water and cutting the stems every day or two. Store more delicate herbs, such as cilantro, oregano, thyme, and dill, by wrapping in a damp paper towel, enclosing in a perforated plastic bag, and refrigerating for up to a week.

Use fresh basil in Pulled Pork Sandwich with Green Mango Slaw (page 121), Corn Risotto with Roasted Cherry Tomatoes (page 135), Smoky Pizza Margherita (page 106), Baked Egg in Fall Vegetables (page 33), and Farfalle with Cantaloupe and Prosciutto (page 141).

Use fresh mint in Pulled Pork Sandwich with Green Mango Slaw (page 121); Farro Salad with Chickpeas, Cherries, and Pecans (page 143); Duck Breast Tacos with Plum Salsa (page 99); Mushroom and Green Garlic Frittata (page 32), and Yogurt Parfait with Rhubarb-Ginger Sauce and Strawberries (page 160). Use fresh parsley in Parsley Garlic Dressing (page 8), Roast Chicken Leg with Gremolata and Sunchokes (page 72), and Spicy Glazed Mini Meatloaf (page 65).

Use fresh cilantro in Yucatan-Style Slow-Roasted Pork (page 66), Pulled Pork Sandwich with Green Mango Slaw (page 121), Duck Breast Tacos with Plum Salsa (page 99), Curried Shrimp on a Sweet Potato (page 46), Mahi Mahi with Kiwi-Avocado Salsa and Coconut Rice (page 79), Cilantro Vinaigrette (page 9), Benedict Rancheros (page 29), Pastoral Tacos (page 91), Cochinita Pibil Tacos with Habanero Salsa (page 95), Shrimp Tacos with Grapefruit–Black Bean Salsa (page 102), Shrimp and Potato Chip Tortilla (page 35), Salsa Verde (page 14), Catfish Tacos with Chipotle Slaw (page 101), Thai Fried Rice with Runny Egg (page 132), and Black Bean Soup with Seared Scallops and Green Salsa (page 54).

Use fresh thyme in Herbed Lemon Confit (page 4), Sweet Potato Soup Base (page 41), and Fall Vegetable Soup with White Beans (page 58).

HALF A LIME

Store it by wrapping it tightly in plastic wrap and refrigerating for 4 to 5 days. Or juice it and freeze the juice in ice cube trays, transfer the cubes to freezer-safe heavy-duty plastic bags, and store in the freezer.

Use in Gingered Chicken Sandwich with Avocado and Mango (page 122); Black Bean Soup with Seared Scallops and Green Salsa (page 54); Thai Fried Rice with Runny Egg (page 132); Roasted Chile Relleno with Avocado-Chipotle Sauce (page 48); Chickpea, Spinach, Feta, and Pepita Tacos (page 89); Duck Breast Tacos with Plum Salsa (page 99); and Pulled Pork Sandwich with Green Mango Slaw (page 121).

continued

ONE-QUARTER TO HALF AN AVOCADO

Store by rubbing the exposed flesh with a little olive oil, then wrapping tightly in plastic wrap, pressing the wrap directly against the flesh of the avocado, and refrigerating for 3 to 4 days. Cut off any browned spots before using.

Use it in Gingered Chicken Sandwich with Avocado and Mango (page 122); Black Bean Soup with Seared Scallops and Green Salsa (page 54); Roasted Chile Relleno with Avocado-Chipotle Sauce (page 48); Chickpea, Spinach, Feta, and Pepita Tacos (page 89); Mahi Mahi with Kiwi-Avocado Salsa and Coconut Rice (page 79), and Avocado, Smoked Oyster, and Pistachio Bruschetta (page 127).

HALF A JALAPEÑO CHILE

Store by drying it thoroughly, wrapping it in plastic wrap, and refrigerating for 3 to 4 days.

Use it in Duck Breast Tacos with Plum Salsa (page 99), Pastoral Tacos (page 91), Mahi Mahi with Kiwi-Avocado Salsa and Coconut Rice (page 79), and Black Bean Soup with Seared Scallops and Green Salsa (page 54).

CELERY STALKS (FROM A BUNCH)

Store by wrapping the remaining bunch in aluminum foil and refrigerating for up to 2 weeks. If you need to recrisp celery, cut off one end and stick it in a glass of ice water for a half hour.

Use it in Sweet Potato Soup Base (page 41), Faux-lognese with Pappardelle (page 140), Spicy Black Bean Soup Base (page 52), or Home-Cooked Beans (page 47).

PART OF A FENNEL BULB

Store by wrapping in a damp paper towel, putting it in a perforated plastic bag, and refrigerating for up to 1 week. It isn't recommended that you freeze fresh fennel.

Use it in Fideos with Sardines and Bread Crumbs (page 149); Smoked Trout, Potato, and Fennel Pizza (page 113); or Red Pepper Chutney (page 17).

PART OF A CAN OF BLACK BEANS, WHITE BEANS, OR CHICKPEAS

Store by draining, rinsing, and transferring to an airtight plastic or glass container. Drizzle with a little olive oil and refrigerate for up to 1 week. To freeze, skip the olive oil step, but cover with water and freeze for several months.

Use the black beans in Benedict Rancheros (page 29), Shrimp Tacos with Grapefruit–Black Bean Salsa (page 102), Peasant's Bowl (page 50), Ex-Texas Salad (page 51), or Roasted Chile Relleno with Avocado-Chipotle Sauce (page 48).

Use the white beans in Fall Vegetable Soup with White Beans (page 58). Use the chickpeas in Farro Salad with Chickpeas, Cherries, and Pecans (page 143); Chickpea, Spinach, Feta, and Pepita Tacos (page 89); Sweet Potato Soup with Chorizo, Chickpeas, and Kale (page 43); and Tuna, Chickpea, and Arugula Sandwich (page 126).

PART OF A CAN OF CRUSHED OR DICED TOMATOES

Transfer the tomatoes with their juices to an airtight plastic or glass container and refrigerate for up to 1 week or freeze for several months.

Use the crushed tomatoes in Benedict Rancheros (page 29), Fideos with Sardines and Bread Crumbs (page 149), Faux-lognese with Pappardelle (page 140); Mushroom and Speck Pizza (page 109), Thai Fried Rice with Runny Egg (page 132), or Chickpea, Spinach, Feta, and Pepita Tacos (page 89).

Use the diced tomatoes in Smoky Pizza Margherita (page 108) or Farro Salad with Chickpeas, Cherries, and Pecans (page 143).

PART OF A CAN OF COCONUT MILK

Store by transferring it to an airtight plastic or glass container. Refrigerate for up to 1 week or freeze in ice cube trays and then transfer to freezer-safe heavy-duty plastic bags and freeze for several months. (It will separate when it thaws, but can be whisked to recombine.)

Use it in Spicy Coconut Sorbet (page 159), Coconut French Toast with Bananas Foster (page 162), and Curried Shrimp on a Sweet Potato (page 46).

PART OF A CAN OF CHIPOTLE IN ADOBO

Store by transferring it to an airtight plastic or glass container. Refrigerate for up to 2 weeks or freeze for several months.

Use it in Roasted Chile Relleno with Avocado-Chipotle Sauce (page 48) or Catfish Tacos with Chipotle Slaw (page 101).

PART OF A BOTTLE OF WINE.

Store by removing as much air as possible from the bottle (use a vacuum device, if possible) and refrigerate for several days, or freeze in ice cube trays, transfer to heavy-duty freezer-safe plastic bags, and freeze for several months.

Use white wine in Corn Risotto with Roasted Cherry Tomatoes (page 135) or Faux-lognese with Pappardelle (page 140), and use white or red wine in Mulled Wine Syrup (page 6).

RÉSERVATION POUR UN

It's a crisp, moonlit night in the Marais, and stylish Parisians are streaming up and down the Rue Sainte Croix de la Bretonnerie. I'm standing, paralyzed, outside the bright blue door of friendly looking little restaurant.

Why on earth can't I bring myself to open it?

This is the first night of my first trip to Paris, and I've come alone, excited to explore the food scene on no one else's itinerary but my own. I've already gobbled up an indulgent lunch of Alsatian choucroute garnie, the smoked pork and cabbage dish, along with beer at a bustling brasserie, and I've done so with nary a speck of self-consciousness.

So why is this any different? Why do I hesitate outside this homey place, staring in and pacing the block instead of going inside?

Because this is not lunch. It's not a cafe where loners write in their journals or read their novels or magazines, and it's not a brasserie, loud with conviviality and communal tables. This is dinner, and I'm convinced that I'll feel conspicuous. I come with neither reservation nor companion, and I see neither free tables nor bar stools on which to wait.

After 20 minutes, my hunger bests my shyness, and I open the door, preparing for blank stares or even that famous French rudeness. I get neither, even after fumbling en français through "For one" and "No, I don't have a reservation." The smiling waiter leads me to a table for two I hadn't seen, next to another single diner I had also overlooked. I'm not alone in my aloneness after all.

Dining solo in Paris, especially at full-fledged restaurants, does require some guts, especially if you're American. A thick skin doesn't hurt either, for those times when a lack of experience with the culture or language leads to the kind of gaffe that'll cause even the politest serveur to roll his eyes.

Maybe it's simply that when you're alone, without a book, newspaper, or conversation to occupy your eyes and mind, you are more apt to notice such reactions, however well hidden. Take my lunch at Au Pied de Cochon, the famous huge restaurant near Les Halles. As I devoured one bracing, sweet-salty oyster after another, I deposited the shells on a small plate on the table. When it was full, a waitress whisked it away—to make room for more shells, I figured. No such luck. I watched as she emptied it at a station, muttered something, and laughed with a coworker, nodding in my direction. She didn't return the plate. I looked over at the neighboring table, where diners were flicking their cigarettes into the equivalent bowl. I had put my oyster shells into, yes, an ashtray.

A thick skin also comes in handy when, inevitably, the service becomes slower for you than for the group of four or six next to you. Attention follows money, understandably I suppose. But that's surely not unique to the City of Light.

At Le Divin, the Marais restaurant where I had my first solo dinner, the waiter asked me to change tables between my honey-rosemary lamb chops and my cheese plate so an entering threesome could get a spot. He was gracious, as was I, but I doubt he would've had the nerve to ask me to move if I had been part of a couple—American, French, or other. There is power in numbers.

And at Bistrot de L'Oulette, a sweet little place also in the Marais, I got plenty of attention when the place was half empty, but once its eight tables were full, I felt as transparent as the champagne cocktail with which I started.

Since that first foray in Paris, I've practiced my solo dining skills on many other travels, and I have to admit, I've not only gotten used to it, but I've also often enjoyed it just as much as eating out with friends. There was the time in Florence when I meant to order a quartino of wine but accidentally got a bottle-sized carafe and felt compelled to drink it all (out of politeness, of course). There was a bar in Venice where I stood sipping espresso, munching on sandwiches, and trying out my bumbling Italian on a policeman, and a homey little place in Puerto Rico whose simple asopao I found so addictive I ate there three nights in a row, something that never would've happened with companions.

Despite the rough spots, I ended up becoming more comfortable dining alone while traveling than I ever will be at home. In Paris, perhaps it was because I got the sense that the French, more so than Americans, understand why someone would go out just for the food, not the company. Perhaps it's because I knew there was no risk of running into anyone I knew—and suffering any pitying response or obligatory invitation to join them.

Or perhaps I just didn't understand what my hosts were really saying about that lone man moaning over his cassoulet and speaking French about as well as a newborn. A year of cooking school may have taught me the difference between canard and quenelles, but in conversations worthy of David Sedaris's book *Me Talk Pretty One Day*, I appear to have asked dozens of people, "Do you speak an English woman?" And they didn't even guffaw. Or if they did, I had no idea, because I'm not sure what a guffaw sounds like in French.

CHAPTER 2
EGGS

· ·

As long as I have eggs, I'm set. Unlike so many other sources of protein, eggs last for weeks in the refrigerator, cook quickly, and come in that perfect portion-controlled package. For a solo cook especially, it's hard not to think of an egg as the perfect food.

I know what you're thinking: What about the cholesterol? Well, plenty of nutritionists think eggs have gotten a bad rap on that count, and they are reminding people that other nutrients in eggs may help lower the risk of heart disease. The consensus seems to be that an egg a day doesn't increase heart disease risk for healthy people and can be part of a nutritious diet.

I've never had better eggs than those from my sister's chickens in southern Maine, where they eat an all-organic diet. Perhaps it's just the placebo effect from knowing that they're backyard-fresh, but those eggs seem creamier and more vibrant tasting, and the yolks stand up high when I fry them. At home, I try to buy eggs only from the farmers' market, partly because of that freshness, but also because I'd rather not support the horrors of industrial poultry.

The funny thing is, I don't tend to eat eggs for breakfast (for me, that's usually a bowl of yogurt and granola). But breakfast for dinner? Bring it on.

BENEDICT RANCHEROS

I love a good corn muffin, and nobody makes one better than Loic Feillet of Panorama Baking in Alexandria, Virginia. The muffin is so good, in fact—moist and studded with chewy little bits of corn—that as soon as I tasted it, I knew I'd incorporate it into an egg dish. The muffin reminded me of an artisanal English muffin, and I just happened to be working on a Mexican variation of eggs Benedict. How perfect! The corn muffin would replace the traditional corn tortilla in huevos rancheros, and I'd poach instead of fry the eggs. Immediately, I had a dish worthy of the muffin, but best of all, even a lesser muffin tastes great when capped off with these ingredients.

1 jalapeno chile
1 teaspoon extra-virgin olive oil
1 small shallot lobe, chopped
1 clove garlic, chopped
1 poblano chile, stemmed, seeded, and chopped
½ teaspoon ground cumin
1 cup canned crushed tomatoes in their juices
½ cup water, plus more as needed
2 eggs

Kosher or sea salt
Freshly cracked black pepper
1 tablespoon finely chopped fresh cilantro leaves
¼ cup cooked black beans, preferably homemade (page 47), rinsed and drained
¼ cup black bean cooking liquid (or water if canned), plus more as needed
1 corn muffin or square of cornbread

Remove the stem from the jalapeño and cut in half lengthwise. Scrape out and reserve the seeds, then finely chop the flesh.

Pour the oil into a medium skillet over medium heat. When the oil starts to shimmer, add the shallot, garlic, poblano, jalapeño flesh, and cumin and cook, stirring occasionally, until the vegetables are tender, 4 to 6 minutes. Add the tomatoes and water and bring to a boil. Decrease the heat to low and let the mixture gently simmer until it has thickened to a saucelike consistency, 5 to 10 minutes.

Meanwhile, poach the eggs following the method described on page 30, keeping them warm by transferring them once they're poached properly to a bowl of 120°F water.

Taste the sauce and add more water, if desired. Season with salt and pepper. If it's not spicy enough, add some of the reserved jalapeño seeds until you reach the desired level of heat. Refrigerate or freeze half of the sauce for another use. Stir the cilantro into the remaining sauce, cover, and remove from the heat.

Pour the beans and their cooking liquid into another small, preferably nonstick skillet set over medium heat. Use a potato masher or a large fork to mash the beans, and let them cook until thickened, 3 to 4 minutes. Add a little liquid if necessary to keep them spreadable, and remove from the heat.

Cut off the domed top of the corn muffin, then cut the muffin in half horizontally. Toast the muffin halves under the broiler or in a toaster oven until golden brown on the cut side.

Transfer the muffins to a plate, cut side up. Spread half the beans on top of each muffin; top with a poached egg and the ranchero sauce. Crumble the reserved muffin top over the sauce, and eat.

Note: This recipe makes twice as much sauce as you need. Before adding the cilantro, refrigerate half of it in an airtight container for up to 1 week or freeze for several months, and use the extra sauce for more Benedict Rancheros another time, on quesadillas or nachos, or whisked with oil and vinegar for a salad dressing.

LOW, SLOW, AND CUSTARDY EGGS

This is a recipe for those of us who are so reverent toward farm-fresh eggs that we'll stand at the stove for almost a half hour, stirring them like a fine risotto. It seems crazy as you're doing it, especially since nothing seems to happen for the first 15 minutes or so, but your perseverance will be rewarded with eggs that have a texture beyond compare, unless you're comparing it to, say, lemon curd, one of the most luxuriously textured foods I know. I refer to eggs done this way as a reverse custard, with more eggs than cream instead of vice versa. I call for the Red Pepper Chutney (page 17) as an accompaniment, but this is such a fabulous way to make eggs, you can combine them with bacon for something even more basic, or you can add any manner of seasonal vegetables, lightly steamed or, better yet, sautéed in butter. If, unlike me, you can't imagine spending this much time on eggs for one, invite a few friends over for brunch, multiply this by four, and try it out on them. You'll see.

2 eggs
2 tablespoons whole milk or half-and-half
Kosher or sea salt
Freshly ground black pepper

1 teaspoon unsalted butter
1 slice rustic bread, toasted
¼ cup Red Pepper Chutney (page 17)

In a small bowl, whisk together the eggs and milk; season with salt and pepper.

Assemble a double boiler, with a couple inches of water in the bottom section, over medium heat. (Don't worry if you don't have a true double boiler; just set a small saucepan with a couple inches of water in it over medium heat and fit a stainless steel bowl that's just slightly larger than the saucepan on top, so that it's airtight. Make sure the bottom of the bowl isn't touching the water.)

When the water in the bottom section of the double-boiler assembly comes to a boil, decrease the heat until the water is just simmering. Add the butter to the top section and let it melt. Pour in the eggs and cook, stirring constantly and slowly with a heatproof spatula, scraping the bottom and sides of the bowl as you stir, until the eggs thicken and form a single large, very soft curd. This will take as long as 20 to 30 minutes; be patient.

When the eggs are very softly set to your liking, lay the toast on to a plate, spoon the eggs on top, top with the chutney, and eat.

THE POACHED EGG

A perfectly poached egg is a beautiful thing, but how do you avoid all those wispy strands that make the egg so stringy and unsightly? There seem to be as many techniques as there are cooks: Some say it's about adding vinegar, but I don't like the taste) that results. Others say it's in the swirling of the water, which helps the egg set quickly and hold its shape.

The culprit behind those wisps is that outer layer of runny albumen. Julia Child dealt with it by first pricking a tiny hole in one end of the egg, then blanching the egg for 15 seconds before cooling, cracking it open, and then poaching. The idea is that the in-the-shell blanching step pre-cooks the thinnest layer of white, leaving the thicker white and yolk unaffected.

Leave it to eminent food scientist Harold McGee to come up with an easier way. Why not just strain out that thin layer of white at the outset? I heard about this from fellow food writer Janet Zimmerman. As soon as I tried it, I knew I was hooked.

THE TECHNIQUE:

1. Line a plate with paper towels.

2. Bring several inches of heavily salted water to a boil in a large sauté pan. Decrease the heat slightly so that the water is bubbling gently but not boiling.

3. Crack the egg into a small dish or ramekin, then pour it into a large slotted spoon held over a small bowl. Swirl the egg around in the spoon so that the thinnest white dribbles between the holes and into the bowl. Rinse the spoon.

4. Tip the egg from the spoon into the bubbling water. Cook it until the white is set but the yolk still wobbles when you press it, 3 to 4 minutes. Use the slotted spoon to transfer the egg to the plate lined with a paper towel. If you want to keep the egg warm for up to 20 minutes or so, transfer it instead to a bowl of very warm (120-degree) water.

THE HARD-COOKED EGG

Like many cooks, I've had many breakthroughs in hard-cooking eggs over the years and have come to a method (or should I say, collection of methods) that works well even with the freshest eggs, which are notoriously difficult to peel.

One breakthrough was the realization, encouraged by my former colleague Sheryl Julian at *The Boston Globe*, that the phrase "hard-boiled" should be banned, because that's the worst way to treat an egg. Lowering the heat to a simmer results in less-rubbery whites. Some cooks even like to leave the eggs sitting in water that's just come off the boil and is off the heat, which also works if you have an extra 10 or 15 minutes. Another discovery, thanks to Tim Ferriss of *The 4-Hour Workweek*, was that a little baking soda in the cooling water makes peeling a breeze.

HERE'S WHAT I DO:

1. Bring several inches of water to a boil in a small saucepan. Decrease the heat to low or medium-low so that the water is gently simmering. Use an egg pricker or thumbtack to make a tiny hole in the rounder end of a large fresh egg, just barely through the shell. Use a slotted spoon to carefully lower the egg into the simmering water.

2. Cook the egg for 9 minutes. While it is cooking, pour 4 cups of cold water into a small bowl, stir in ½ teaspoon baking soda, and add 1 to 2 cups ice.

3. When the egg is finished cooking, remove it with the slotted spoon and transfer it to the ice water. Let it sit in the water for about 30 seconds. As soon as it's cool enough to handle, reach in and remove it with one hand. Quickly but gently crack it all over against the countertop, then peel off a little from the round end and return the egg to the water. After another minute or two, remove the egg and easily slip off the peel.

MUSHROOM AND GREEN GARLIC FRITTATA

I spend a bundle on mushrooms from a bountiful display at the Dupont Circle FreshFarm Market just about every Sunday—but not in the summer. That's because mushrooms are available practically year-round (many of them are cultivated), while tomatoes, corn, broccoli, and the like have a shorter season. So I reserve my mushroom purchases for when the bulk of the other seasonal produce has faded or hasn't quite arrived. In the spring, I love to combine them with one of the items I spend all winter looking forward to: green garlic, basically an immature form of the plant, picked before it has fully formed its bulbous collection of cloves. You can use the whole thing like a leek or green onion (both of them in the same family), but it has the addictive taste of fresh, pungent garlic throughout. Since I also associate spring with eggs, I like to pair them with mushrooms and green garlic in a simple frittata. If you can't find green garlic or want to make this in another season, feel free to substitute a small leek. Eat this frittata with a side dish, such as salad, bread, and/or hash browns, for a filling meal.

2 eggs
1 tablespoon Greek-style yogurt
Kosher or sea salt
Freshly ground black pepper
1 teaspoon extra-virgin olive oil
2 ounces cremini, button, or other mushroom of your choice, chopped (about ½ cup)

1 green garlic bulb and stalk, white and light green parts, thinly sliced
1 teaspoon unsalted butter
1 tablespoon freshly grated Parmigiano-Reggiano cheese
4 large mint leaves, stacked, rolled, and thinly sliced

Preheat the broiler with the rack about 4 to 5 inches from the flame or element.

In a small bowl, whisk together the eggs and yogurt; season with salt and pepper.

In a small ovenproof skillet, such as cast iron, heat the olive oil over medium heat. When it shimmers, add the mushrooms and green garlic. Cook, stirring occasionally, until the mushrooms exude their juices and the green garlic is tender and starts to brown, 4 to 5 minutes. Transfer the mushrooms and green garlic to a plate.

Plop the butter into the skillet and let it melt and foam up. As soon as the foam starts to subside, pour in the eggs and swirl the pan so the eggs reach the edges. Let the eggs cook, undisturbed, until they are set on the bottom, about 2 minutes. Scatter the mushrooms, green garlic, and Parmigiano-Reggiano on top and transfer to the broiler.

Broil for just a minute or two, until the surface of the frittata is set. Remove, transfer to a plate, sprinkle with the mint, and eat.

BAKED EGG in FALL VEGETABLES

The payoff for having made the Stewed Cauliflower, Butternut Squash, and Tomatoes (page 55), beyond that first bowl of pasta I hope you had with it, is that you can use it for quick treatments such as this one. With its runny yolk enriching the vegetables, it's a satisfying breakfast dish on its own, or it can morph into a brunch or breakfast-for-dinner dish with the addition of crusty bread and a side salad.

1 teaspoon unsalted butter, at room temperature
²/₃ cup Stewed Cauliflower, Butternut Squash, and
  Tomatoes (page 55), cold
1 egg
Kosher or sea salt

1 tablespoon dried bread crumbs
3 large basil leaves, finely chopped
1 tablespoon freshly grated Parmigiano-Reggiano
  cheese

Preheat the oven to 375°F. Coat the inside of a large (8-ounce) ramekin with the butter.

Add ⅓ cup of the vegetables to the ramekin and make a well in the center of the vegetables with a teaspoon. Carefully break the egg into the well, season with salt, and top with the remaining ⅓ cup stewed vegetables.

Mix the bread crumbs with the basil and sprinkle evenly on top of the vegetables; sprinkle the cheese on top.

Bake for 20 to 25 minutes, until the topping is browned and crisp, and when you use a spoon to gently lift some of the vegetables from the top to uncover the egg, you can see that the white is cooked through but the yolk is still runny.

Let cool for a few minutes, then eat with a spoon.

SWISS CHARD, BACON, AND GOAT CHEESE OMELET

Try as I might, I just couldn't leave the bacon out of this omelet. Obviously, nothing goes better with eggs. But beyond that, bacon gives the slightly bitter chard an addictive smoky and, well, meaty flavor, while the goat cheese offsets it all with a tart creaminess. The result: a hearty, one-dish meal.

2 eggs
Kosher or sea salt
Freshly ground black pepper
2 or 3 Swiss chard leaves

1 slice bacon, cut into ¼-inch slices
1 small shallot lobe, thinly sliced
1 teaspoon extra-virgin olive oil
1 ounce soft goat cheese, cut into small pieces

In a small bowl, whisk the eggs to combine and season generously with salt and pepper.

Remove the Swiss chard leaves from the stems, and discard the stems or save them for another use. Stack the leaves, roll, and thinly slice. (You should have about ½ cup lightly packed leaves.)

Set a small skillet, well-seasoned cast iron or nonstick, over medium heat, and scatter the bacon and shallot in the pan. Cook, stirring occasionally, until the bacon is crisp and the shallot slices are lightly browned and tender, 3 or 4 minutes. Add the Swiss chard and cook until the chard is wilted and shrunk, stirring occasionally, another few minutes. Transfer the chard-bacon mixture to a plate.

Return the pan to medium heat and pour in the olive oil. When it shimmers, pour in the eggs, swirling and tilting the pan so that the eggs fill the pan. Let the eggs cook undisturbed until the bottom is just set, 1 to 2 minutes. With a spatula, carefully lift one edge of the eggs and tilt the pan so that the loose eggs run underneath.

Scatter the chard-bacon mixture on one side of the omelet and top with the goat cheese. Use a spatula to quickly lift the omelet from the other side and fold it over.

Transfer the omelet to a plate, and eat.

SHRIMP AND POTATO CHIP TORTILLA

I don't make a habit of having potato chips in the house, because I really don't have much self-control around them. But when I read in Anya von Bremzen's go-to cookbook, *The New Spanish Table*, that chef-genius Ferran Adrià makes a tortilla de patatas (that glorious traditional Spanish omelet) with potato chips, I was tempted to buy some. That same year, 2005, my friend, chef José Andrés, a protégé of Adrià's, also included a potato-chip tortilla recipe in his energetic book, *Tapas: A Taste of Spain in America*, so the decision was obvious. It turns out that this humblest of dishes, one of my favorites when I traveled in Spain, was perfectly easy to scale down to single-serving size. To justify its place on my dinner table, though, I added shrimp to make it a meal. Eat with a green salad or other crisp vegetables on the side. If desired, spoon some Red Pepper Chutney (page 17) on top.

2 eggs
Kosher or sea salt
Freshly ground black pepper
¼ teaspoon pimenton (smoked Spanish paprika)
1 (1-ounce) bag potato chips, preferably kettle-cooked and lightly salted

4 teaspoons extra-virgin olive oil, plus more as needed
1 medium shallot lobe, thinly sliced
Leaves from 4 or 5 sprigs cilantro, chopped
4 or 5 medium shrimp (about 2 ounces), peeled, deveined, and halved crosswise

In a small bowl, whisk together the eggs, a light sprinkling of salt and pepper, and the pimenton.

Lightly crush the potato chips in the bag. Stir them into the eggs and let the mixture sit until the potato chips are soft, 5 to 10 minutes.

Pour 2 teaspoons of the oil into a very small skillet over medium heat. When the oil starts to shimmer, add the shallot. Cook, stirring occasionally, until the shallot is soft and starts to brown, 3 to 4 minutes. Use a slotted spoon to transfer the shallot to a plate to cool.

When cool, stir the shallot into the egg mixture. Stir in the cilantro and shrimp until thoroughly combined.

With the skillet still over medium heat, pour in the remaining 2 teaspoons oil. When it starts to shimmer, pour in the tortilla mixture. Let it cook undisturbed for a minute or two, then shake the pan back and forth and run a thin spatula around the edges of the tortilla. If there is loose, runny egg, lift an edge of the tortilla with the spatula and tilt the pan to let the liquid egg run underneath. Cook until the top of the tortilla is still wet but no longer a runny liquid, 3 to 5 minutes or longer, depending on the size of

the pan. Run the spatula around the edges of the tortilla and then all the way underneath it to make sure the bottom is not sticking.

If your spatula is large enough, use it to flip the tortilla in the pan. Alternatively, take a plate slightly larger than the skillet, and invert it on top of the skillet. Using oven mitts, grab both sides of the skillet, also holding the plate, and quickly and decisively turn both skillet and plate upside down, inverting the tortilla onto the plate and removing the skillet.

If the skillet looks dry, add another teaspoon or so of olive oil, and when it starts to shimmer, slide the tortilla back into the skillet, uncooked side down. Shake the skillet to straighten the tortilla, decrease the heat to low, and continue cooking until a skewer inserted into the center comes out dry, 2 to 3 minutes.

Invert the tortilla onto a plate again, let it cool for a few minutes, and eat.

Note: If you don't have a very small skillet, this will still work; it won't be as thick as a Spanish tortilla and will instead be closer to a frittata.

PUFFY DUCK EGG FRITTATA
WITH SMOKED SALMON

I'll admit to a tendency toward obsession, especially when it comes to food, as my experience with duck eggs proves. I bought my first dozen a few years ago at the Saturday farmers' market at 14th and U Streets in Washington, D.C., and from the first time I fried one, I was pretty much hooked, buying duck eggs and only duck eggs and going through a dozen every week or two, at least while the ducks were laying. I've since veered back toward moderation, especially after remembering that these richer, more flavorful eggs are also higher in saturated fat and much higher in cholesterol. Still, I like to splurge every now and then, and this puffy frittata is one of my favorite ways. It also illustrates the magical properties of egg whites as a leavener; the simple process of separating whites from yolks, beating the whites to the soft-peak stage, and folding the two together results in a light-as-air texture, something between a frittata and a soufflé. Nonetheless, you can use these same ingredients in a more straightforward frittata; instead of separating the eggs, just follow the method for the Mushroom and Green Garlic Frittata (page 32). And if you can't find duck eggs, chicken eggs work fine here, too.

2 large duck eggs, separated
Kosher or sea salt
Freshly ground black pepper
1 tablespoon unsalted butter

2 ounces smoked salmon, cut into thin ribbons
    or chunks (about 1/3 cup)
1 tablespoon fresh chives, cut into 1/2-inch pieces
1 to 2 tablespoons Greek-style yogurt

Preheat the broiler with the rack set about 4 to 5 inches from the flame or element.

Using a handheld or stand mixer fitted with the whisk attachment on high speed, beat the egg whites for several minutes until they foam, thicken, and make soft peaks when you turn off the mixer and lift the beaters.

In a separate bowl, whisk the yolks with a fork to break them up, and season generously with salt and pepper. Add a third of the egg whites to the egg yolks, stirring to lighten and combine, then gently fold the remaining egg whites into the egg yolks, being careful not to overmix and deflate the whites.

Set a small ovenproof skillet over medium heat. Add the butter, swirling to coat the pan and letting the butter melt and foam up. As soon as the foam starts to subside, pour in the egg mixture, tilting the pan to make sure the egg covers the bottom. Let it cook undisturbed until the bottom is just set, approximately 1 to 2 minutes.

Quickly scatter the salmon on top of the eggs and sprinkle with the chives. Transfer the skillet to the broiler and let the eggs cook until the surface has set, 1 to 2 minutes.

Transfer to a plate, top with dollops of the yogurt, and eat.

CHAPTER 3
SWEET POTATOES, BEANS, and OTHER VEGGIES

Like many a health- and earth-conscious eater, I'm trying to put vegetables closer to the center of my diet, cooking more vegetarian (or at least plant-focused) dishes throughout the week. It can require a little more planning, because most produce doesn't freeze as well as meat, poultry, and even some seafood does, but it's worth the effort.

At the top of the list of my favorites is the humble sweet potato. On many a night, in fact, my just-home-from-work drill goes like this: Drop bag, turn on oven, put in sweet potato, take dog to park, return, remove sweet potato, slash, squeeze, season, eat. Time was, I ate them with a salad and/or piece of protein on the side, until I started concocting special toppings just for them.

Running a close second are beans: black beans and chickpeas, particularly, but also pinto beans, cannellini, and others, most of the time cooked from dried, and often used in other dishes or as the base of soups.

With both those items lasting so long in my pantry, I can save my refrigerator for the more delicate fresh produce that makes it home with me every week from one of the nearby farmers' markets or, in season, from my little community-garden plot.

SHOPPING

Grocery stores have traditionally been pretty inhospitable places for single cooks, but the landscape is changing. Realizing the buying power of more than 31 million Americans, some savvy stores, particularly in urban areas, are getting wise to the fact that some of us just want to buy a few broccoli florets, a half-dozen eggs, even a half-bottle of wine.

In the produce aisle, though, celery seems to be one of the last holdouts. When have you seen a recipe call for more than just a stalk or two (and that's for dishes that serve four)? And when have you seen it sold in a supermarket in anything less than a large bunch—or perhaps a package of several celery hearts? It's no wonder smart cooks have long scoured stores' salad bars for smaller amounts of such items, realizing that a higher by-the-pound price for something already chopped is compensated by the fact that you buy what you plan to use—no more, no less.

Sometimes I think I should start up a single-cook's buying club, where we go to the store to shop in groups and then carve up items like heads of cauliflower, bunches of celery, clamshell packs of herbs, and family packs of pork chops right there in the parking lot. Until I get that going, though, here are some things to keep in mind.

1. If you want something in a smaller quantity, ask for it to be divided. That's the only way the store will know that you and other single cooks have unique needs, and the only way they'll start paying attention. Ask the butcher to cut the 6-pound pork shoulder in half, tell the cheesemonger you want just 2 or 3 ounces of that aged gouda, plead with the bread counter to cut off a hunk of that sourdough boule. Harangue the produce guy about why the celery is sold by the bunch and not the pound, and maybe he'll let you treat it like the bananas and pull off a stalk or two.

2. Think about what freezes well and what doesn't, and recognize the fine line between convenient and indulgent. I'm thinking of meats here. Many stores now sell chicken, pork, and beef in the form of pounded-out cutlets, which are sized just right for the single chef and cook in a flash. But they can cost 30 percent more than whole breasts and boneless chops, which you can easily pound out yourself, wrap in plastic wrap, and freeze individually.

3. It may sound obvious, but look for smaller versions (or relatives) of your favorite produce. Unless I'm cooking a larger quantity of something, I gravitate toward shallots over onions, for instance. That helps me avoid the problem of having a leftover onion half. Buy small new potatoes rather than huge Idahos, and baby bok choy over the full-size version.

4. Patronize your local farmers' market. Farmers sell many more varieties of produce and at different stages of life, meaning you're much more likely to see small versions of melons, squashes, tomatoes, and more. Better yet, you can almost always buy as little of something as you'd like, because so many farmers sell by the pound rather than the bunch. Even if they don't, the personal relationships that the market atmosphere facilitates means they're more likely to make an exception once you start a conversation going.

5. Grow your own. Even if you don't have garden space, grow pots of herbs on your windowsill that you can clip from as needed.

SWEET POTATO SOUP BASE

Makes about 4 cups

I got the idea from Lidia Bastianich to make soup bases that pack a lot of flavor on the weekend, then freeze them and thaw them as needed, adding various ingredients on the fly to take them in different directions. I like to concentrate the base, which saves freezer space, and then thin it out when I make a finished soup. Before you thin it out (and jazz it up) for the final soup, this base may remind you of a certain fluffy Thanksgiving side dish (minus the mini-marshmallows, thankfully), but there are some key differences. Besides the lack of cream or sugar, the most important one is the cooking method: Rather than boiling peeled cubes of sweet potato, I like to roast them, concentrating the complex flavor, which is highlighted by subtle hints of thyme and curry. This makes an especially vibrant backdrop to such treatments as Sweet Potato Soup with Chorizo, Chickpeas, and Kale (page 43). There are many other possibilities. You can sprinkle ground chipotle or pimenton (smoked Spanish paprika) for heat and/or smoke, or add toasted pecans, yogurt (or sour cream or crème fraîche), and other sausages or cured meats.

2 (10- to 12-ounce) sweet potatoes
2 tablespoons extra-virgin olive oil
2 carrots, peeled and thinly sliced
1 celery stalk, thinly sliced
1 small leek, white and pale greens, thinly sliced

2 sprigs thyme
Kosher or sea salt
Pinch of curry powder
2 cups light chicken or vegetable stock, warmed

Preheat the oven to 425°F.

Use a fork or sharp knife to prick the sweet potatoes in several places. Place on a piece of aluminum foil and bake until the sweet potatoes are tender and can be easily squeezed, 60 to 75 minutes. (Alternatively, to speed up the process, microwave the pricked sweet potatoes on High for 1 minute, then carefully transfer to the oven on a piece of foil. Bake until the potatoes are tender, 30 to 45 minutes.)

Pour the oil into a 3-quart saucepan over medium heat. When it starts to shimmer, add the carrots, celery, leek, thyme, and a pinch of salt. Stir to combine well, then decrease the heat to low, cover the pot, and allow the vegetables to sweat in their own juices until very soft, 10 to 15 minutes. (Take care not to allow the vegetables to burn.)

Scrape into the saucepan the soft flesh from the roasted sweet potatoes, add the curry powder, and stir to combine, mashing the sweet potato flesh with a spoon. The mixture will be chunky. Stir in the stock

and combine well. Bring the mixture to a boil, then decrease the heat so the mixture gently simmers, and cook, covered but with the lid slightly ajar, for about 15 minutes to let the flavors meld. Allow the mixture to cool slightly, then remove and discard the thyme.

Use a handheld immersion blender to puree the soup base, which will be very thick. (Alternatively, you can puree it in a blender or food processor. If using a blender, be sure to remove the center cap on the lid and cover with a dish towel to let steam escape, and work in small batches to avoid splattering the soup.) Taste and add salt if needed.

Let the soup base cool to room temperature. Divide it into 4 portions and use immediately, refrigerate for up to 2 weeks, or freeze in small containers or heavy-duty freezer-safe resealable plastic bags, pressing as much air out of the bag as possible before sealing. It will keep frozen for several months.

SWEET POTATO SOUP with CHORIZO, CHICKPEAS, and KALE

Turn the Sweet Potato Soup Base into a meal with spicy chorizo, hearty chickpeas, and vibrant green kale. This makes a truly beautiful bowl of soup. If you'd rather keep this soup vegetarian, try the grain-based chorizo substitute from Field Roast, one of the first meat substitutes I've actually liked. It's available in natural food stores in almost every state and through www.fieldroast.com.

1 cup Sweet Potato Soup Base (page 41), defrosted if frozen

½ to ¾ cup water or vegetable stock

1 (3- or 4-ounce) link fresh Mexican chorizo

⅓ cup cooked chickpeas, preferably homemade (page 47), rinsed and drained

4 or 5 leaves Tuscan kale (sometimes called black, dinosaur, or lacinato kale), stripped from the stem and torn into bite-size pieces

Pour the soup base into a small saucepan over medium heat. Whisk in ½ cup of the water and cook until the soup is bubbling hot, 3 to 4 minutes. Add more water if you want the soup thinner. Reduce the heat to low, cover, and keep it hot.

Heat a medium skillet over medium-high heat. Slice through the chorizo casing and squeeze the sausage into the skillet. Cook, breaking it up with a spoon,

until the chorizo's fat starts to melt, 1 to 2 minutes. Add the chickpeas and cook until the chorizo and chickpeas brown, 4 to 6 minutes. Add the kale and stir-fry until the kale wilts slightly and brightens in color, 1 to 2 minutes.

Pour the soup base into a soup bowl, top with the chorizo mixture, and eat.

SWEET POTATO AND ORANGE SOUP WITH SMOKY PECANS

. . . .

This elegant soup has a depth of flavor, brightened by orange and layered with smoked paprika, that would make it right at home as a dinner party starter. For yourself, pair it with a side salad and a big piece of crusty bread, and it's dinner tonight, while you plan the party for another day.

. . . .

1 cup Sweet Potato Soup Base (page 41), defrosted if frozen
¼ cup freshly squeezed orange juice
¼ cup water or vegetable stock, plus more as needed
Kosher or sea salt
2 tablespoons pecan halves

1 tablespoon extra-virgin olive oil
½ teaspoon pimentón (smoked Spanish paprika) or ground chipotle chile
2 tablespoons crème fraîche or sour cream, whisked until smooth
Finely grated zest of 1 orange

Pour the soup base into a small saucepan over medium heat. Whisk in the orange juice and water, adding more water if you want a thinner consistency. Cook until the soup is bubbling hot, 3 to 4 minutes. Taste and add salt if needed. Decrease the heat to low, cover, and keep it hot.

Heat a small skillet over medium-high heat. Add the pecans and cook, stirring occasionally, until they are fragrant and start to darken, 2 to 3 minutes. Pour in the oil, stir in the pimentón, and cook for another 30 seconds to dissolve the spice. Use a heatproof spatula to scrape the spiced oil and pecans into a small bowl.

Pour the soup into a serving bowl, dollop the crème fraîche in the middle, and top with the pecans and spiced oil. Sprinkle the orange zest on top, and eat.

MISO PORK ON A SWEET POTATO

When I visited Tokyo and Kyoto with my friend Devra a couple years back, I didn't want to leave. I would say it was the beautiful aesthetic, the attention to design and style, the amazingly efficient trains, but really, of course, it was the food. I was especially excited when I learned how much the Japanese revere the sweet potato, one of my all-time favorite foods. In season (fall and winter), street vendors hawk stone-roasted ones—paler-fleshed and sweeter than ours. Famous cookbook author Harumi Kurihara showed me how she loves to mash miso into roasted sweet potatoes, so when I returned home, I knew that even the orange-fleshed varieties here would take beautifully to Japanese flavors. For a kick of bitterness that nicely offsets the earthy miso, use broccoli rabe instead of the broccolini.

1 small sweet potato (about 6 ounces)
2 teaspoons extra-virgin olive oil
3 ounces lean ground pork
4 or 5 stalks (6 ounces) broccolini (or substitute broccoli rabe), cut into ¾-inch pieces
1 tablespoon white miso

2 tablespoons water, plus more as needed
1 scallion, white and green parts, thinly sliced on the diagonal
Asian-style hot sauce, such as Sriracha sauce, for drizzling (optional)

Preheat the oven to 425°F.

Use a fork or sharp knife to prick the sweet potato in several places. Place on a piece of aluminum foil and bake until the sweet potato is tender and can be easily squeezed, 40 to 60 minutes. (Alternatively, to speed up the process, the pricked sweet potato can be microwaved on High for 1 minute, then carefully transferred to the oven on a piece of foil. Bake until the potato is tender, 25 to 35 minutes.)

Meanwhile, pour the oil into a medium skillet over medium-high heat. Add the pork and stir-fry until no traces of pink remain and the pork starts to exude juices, about 5 minutes, breaking up any large clumps as you cook. Add the broccolini and stir-fry until the vegetables are barely tender and retain some crunch, 3 to 4 minutes. Add the miso and

water; cook, stirring, for 1 minute or so, until a sauce forms. If the mixture seems dry, add up to a few more tablespoons of water, stirring to combine.

When the sweet potato has finished baking, place it on a serving plate. Use a knife to slash open the sweet potato, then spoon the miso-pork mixture on top. Sprinkle with the scallion, drizzle with a little Sriracha, and eat while it's hot.

Note: You can roast more than one sweet potato at a time and keep it, wrapped in aluminum foil or plastic, in the refrigerator for up to 1 week before reheating it in a low oven or in the microwave while you make the topping. If you can't find a sweet potato this small, feel free to roast one twice the size (it will take longer, obviously), and just cut it in half.

CURRIED SHRIMP ON A SWEET POTATO

This potato topper was inspired by Polynesian and Southeast Asian combinations of shrimp and mashed sweet potatoes. A good-quality Indian curry powder can be substituted for the Thai curry paste.

1 small sweet potato (about 6 ounces)
2 teaspoons extra-virgin olive oil
½-inch piece fresh ginger, peeled and thinly sliced
¼ medium red bell pepper, cut into very thin strips (about ¼ cup total)
1 teaspoon Thai red curry paste (or substitute good-quality Indian curry powder)

3 tablespoons coconut milk
4 ounces any size shrimp, peeled, deveined, and cut into ½-inch pieces
Kosher or sea salt
Finely chopped fresh cilantro leaves

Preheat the oven to 425°F.

Use a fork or sharp knife to prick the sweet potato in several places. Place on a piece of aluminum foil and bake until the sweet potato is tender and can be easily squeezed, 40 to 60 minutes. (Alternatively, to speed up the process, the pricked sweet potato can be microwaved on High for 1 minute, then carefully transferred to the oven on a piece of foil. Bake until the potato is tender, 25 to 35 minutes.)

Meanwhile, heat the oil in a small heavy skillet over medium heat. When the oil shimmers, toss in the ginger and sauté until it becomes very fragrant and starts to soften, 2 to 3 minutes. Add the bell pepper and cook just until the strips lose their crunch, 2 to 4 minutes. Decrease the heat to medium-low and add the curry paste and coconut milk, stirring to thoroughly combine. Add the shrimp and stir to incorporate. Cook just until the shrimp are firm and opaque, 1 to 2 minutes. Season with salt to taste; remove from the heat.

When the sweet potato has finished baking, place it on a serving plate. Slash it open with a sharp knife. Spoon on the shrimp mixture, sprinkle with the cilantro, and eat.

Note: Feel free to roast more than one sweet potato at a time and keep it, wrapped in aluminum foil or plastic, in the refrigerator for up to 1 week before reheating in a low oven or in the microwave while you make the topping. If you can't find a sweet potato this small, roast one twice the size (it will take longer, obviously), and cut it in half before topping.

HOME-COOKED BEANS

Makes 4 to 6 cups

Beans certainly hold up better in the industrial canning process than many other vegetables, but there are still many good reasons to cook your own, not the least of which is the fact that so many canned varieties come packed with way more sodium than you need.

Here's my adaptation of bean maven Steve Sando's basic stovetop method for cooking beans. If you have a pressure cooker or a slow cooker, feel free to experiment with it. This recipe gives the beans a relatively neutral seasoning that leaves them easy to take in different directions. If desired, you can add herbs and spices (torn dried chile peppers, toasted and ground cumin seeds, black peppercorns, oregano) to the cooking liquid, but resist the urge to add anything acidic, such as tomatoes, citrus, or vinegar, until the beans are cooked, or the skins of the beans will not soften as they should.

1 pound dry beans of any variety
1 tablespoon extra-virgin olive oil
1 carrot, peeled and cut into 1-inch pieces
1 celery stalk, cut into 1-inch pieces

1 small yellow or white onion, cut into 1-inch pieces
2 large cloves garlic, smashed
2 teaspoons fine sea salt, or more to taste

Rinse the beans, picking through them to remove any debris. Pour them into a bowl and add enough water to cover them by about 1 inch. Soak for at least 6 hours and preferably overnight.

Pour the oil into a medium pot over medium heat. When it starts to shimmer, add the carrot, celery, onion, and garlic. Cook until the vegetables start to soften, 5 to 6 minutes. Add the beans and their soaking liquid, and add more water as needed to cover by about 1 inch.

Increase the heat to medium-high and bring to a boil. Reduce the heat to low or medium-low so that the liquid barely simmers, cover, and cook the beans until tender, 1 to 2 hours (or even longer, depending on the variety and age of the beans).

Add the salt, and cook for another 10 or 20 minutes so that the beans absorb the salt. Taste, and add more salt if needed. Whatever you're not using immediately, cool to room temperature and refrigerate in an airtight container for up to 2 weeks, or portion into heavy-duty freezer-safe plastic bags and freeze for several months.

DRIED BEANS

Talk to Rancho Gordo owner Steve Sando about beans, and he'll change the way you think about them. Buy his heirloom beans, and it's hard to go back to supermarket varieties. Sando's beans differ from most supermarket beans by virtue of age: His beans are sold within a year of harvesting, while supermarket beans can be many years old. Age matters: The older the beans, the longer it takes to cook them. Besides being out-and-out delicious, Rancho Gordo beans also retain their shape wonderfully. If you don't want to wait for Steve's beans to arrive by mail order, seek out other heirloom beans if possible, or buy them from a market that sells beans in bulk and replenishes the supply frequently.

ROASTED CHILE RELLENO
WITH **AVOCADO-CHIPOTLE SAUCE**

For the longest time, chile relleno was my favorite dish, and, really, what's not to like? A cheese-stuffed poblano pepper, battered and fried, with a spicy sauce? Bring it on, right? Making it at home was a different story: Dipping that delicate pepper in the batter without the stuffing falling out was, well, beyond me. This version may seem involved, but believe me, compared to the traditional version, it's positively streamlined. I like an almost burrito-like filling, with starchy rice or farro included, but there's no egg binder, no batter, no oil to heat up (and splatter everywhere). It's oven-roasted and vegetarian, but spicy and cheesy all the same. Eat with a small salad if you like.

1 large poblano pepper

FILLING
2 teaspoons extra-virgin olive oil
½ teaspoon ground ancho chile
1 medium shallot lobe, thinly sliced
1 clove garlic, thinly sliced
4 or 5 Swiss chard leaves, stacked, rolled, and thinly sliced
1 plum or other small tomato, cored, seeded, and chopped
¼ cup cooked black beans, preferably homemade (page 47), rinsed and drained
¼ cup cooked brown or white rice or farro (see page 143)

1 ounce Monterey Jack cheese, cut into small chunks or grated
Kosher or sea salt

SAUCE
½ avocado, pitted
2 tablespoons low-fat yogurt
¼ teaspoon adobo sauce (from a can of chipotle in adobo)
Juice of ½ lime
2 to 3 tablespoons water
1 tablespoon roasted shelled pumpkin seeds (pepitas)

Preheat the oven to 400°F.

Blacken the skin of the poblano pepper by turning a gas burner to high and setting the poblano right on the grate, using tongs to turn it periodically until it is charred all over. (If you don't have a gas stove, preheat your oven broiler and set the poblano on a pan about 4 to 5 inches from the broiler element or flame and broil for 5 to 6 minutes, turning periodically until it is charred all over.) Transfer the pepper to a stainless steel or glass bowl, cover with plastic wrap, and let steam as it cools.

While the poblano is cooling, make the filling. Pour the olive oil into a medium skillet over medium heat. When the oil starts to shimmer, sprinkle in the ground ancho chile and cook for about 30 seconds, until it foams and releases its aroma. Add the shallot and garlic and cook, stirring occasionally, until the vegetables start to soften, 2 to 4 minutes. Stir in the Swiss chard and tomato and cook until the chard wilts and the tomato softens, 4 to 5 minutes. Transfer to a small bowl. Stir in the black beans, rice, and cheese, and season with salt to taste. Let cool.

When the poblano is cool enough to handle, gently rub off the blackened skin, being careful not to tear the flesh open. Use a sharp paring knife to cut a slit on one side of the poblano, starting near the stem and cutting about halfway down the side. Carefully reach in and remove the seeds, trying not to enlarge the opening if possible. Use your hands to carefully stuff the filling into the poblano, getting it as full as possible. Carefully transfer the stuffed poblano to a baking sheet, cut side up. Don't worry if the filling is exposed.

Roast the poblano for 15 to 20 minutes, until the filling is bubbling and the cheese is melted.

While the poblano is roasting, make the sauce. Scoop the avocado flesh into a small bowl and use a fork to thoroughly mash it. Whisk in the yogurt,

adobo sauce, lime juice, and 2 tablespoons of water, adding more water if you want the sauce to be thinner.

When the poblano has finished roasting, transfer it to a dinner plate and let it cool for a few minutes. Then spoon the sauce on top, sprinkle with the pumpkin seeds, and eat.

Note: To roast the pumpkin seeds, spread them in a single layer on a baking sheet. Bake at 375°F for 5 to 7 minutes, until the seeds are very fragrant. Immediately transfer to a plate to stop the cooking and allow the seeds to cool completely.

PEASANT'S BOWL

One of my college hangouts was a scruffy Austin restaurant called Les Amis, which my friends and I called "Lazy Me," in honor of the decidedly unhelpful service. The food was dependable even if the waitstaff wasn't, and a standby for me was a simple bowl of black beans, rice, and cheese, priced so even students without trust funds could afford it. Later, I learned that the combination of beans and rice is one of the most nutritionally complete vegetarian meals possible. While beans are one of the vegetables that takes better to canning than others, if you make a pot of your own from scratch (page 47), the taste and texture are incomparable. When Les Amis finally closed, torn down to make room for a new Starbucks, I missed not just the peasant's bowl, but those inattentive waitresses, too.

2 teaspoons extra-virgin olive oil
½ teaspoon ground cumin
¼ teaspoon ground ancho chile
¼ teaspoon dried oregano (preferably Mexican)
1 clove garlic, thinly sliced
1 small shallot lobe, thinly sliced
¾ cup cooked black beans, preferably homemade (page 47), with ½ cup cooking liquid or ½ cup vegetable stock

Kosher or sea salt
1 cup cooked brown rice
1 ounce Monterey Jack, Cheddar, or feta cheese, shredded or crumbled
1 small tomato, cored, seeded, and chopped
1 scallion, white and green parts, thinly sliced
A few dashes hot pepper sauce, such as Tabasco

Pour the oil into a medium skillet over medium heat. When it starts to shimmer, sprinkle in the cumin and ground ancho, swirling the pan and cooking until the spices bubble up and become very fragrant, about 30 seconds.

Add the oregano, garlic, and shallot and sauté until they become tender, about 3 or 4 minutes.

Pour in the black beans and their cooking liquid, stir to combine, and cook until the beans are hot and the liquid has thickened, just 2 or 3 minutes for home-cooked beans and a little longer for canned beans and stock. Add salt to taste, decrease the heat to low, and keep warm.

Warm the rice by microwaving it on high heat for 30 seconds. Spoon it into a large dinner bowl. Use a spoon to push the rice to the edges of the plate and create an indentation for the beans.

Spoon the beans and their liquid into the center of the rice, top with the cheese, tomato, scallion, and Tabasco to taste, and eat.

EX-TEXAS SALAD

When I was growing up, one of my mother's holiday specialties was something she called "Texas Salad," similar to something others call taco salad, although hers didn't include ground beef. It was basically a head of iceberg lettuce, a couple cans of pinto beans, a block of Cheddar cheese, a bag of Fritos, and a whole bottle of Catalina French-style dressing, along with a red onion and a tomato or two. Okay, here's my confession: I loved it, the first day more than the second (although others in my family would say the reverse). My tastes have gotten a little more sophisticated since then, but I still appreciate what my Mom was going for: sweet and sour, crunchy and fresh, a little protein, and a little fat. I've had fun updating it, but, Mom, you'll notice, I've kept all your principles intact.

2 tablespoons peanut oil
1 corn tortilla, preferably homemade (page 84)
2 cups packed, torn romaine lettuce leaves
½ cup cooked black beans, preferably homemade (page 47), rinsed and drained
1 scallion, white and green parts, thinly sliced on the diagonal

2 ounces feta cheese, crumbled
2 large pieces 12-Hour Tomatoes (page 2), drained
2 tablespoons Cilantro Vinaigrette (page 9)

Line a plate with paper towels. Pour the oil into a small skillet over medium-heat. When it starts to shimmer, add the tortilla and fry it on each side until crispy and golden brown, 1 to 2 minutes. Transfer the tortilla to the paper towel–lined plate. When it cools, break it up into bite-size pieces.

In a large bowl, toss the lettuce with the tortilla pieces, black beans, scallion, feta, tomatoes, and vinaigrette, and eat.

Note: If you don't have 12-Hour Tomatoes (page 2) in your refrigerator, you can substitute 3 or 4 oil-packed sun-dried tomatoes.

SPICY BLACK BEAN SOUP BASE

Makes 4 to 5 cups

• •

It doesn't make a lot of sense to make just enough soup for one serving, especially when the soup is based on long-cooking beans. But that doesn't mean solo cooks have to go without their soup fix. This base uses two of my favorite ingredients, black beans and ancho chiles, to provide the backdrop for Black Bean Tortilla Soup with Shrimp (on page 53) and Black Bean Soup with Seared Scallops and Green Salsa (page 54). But that's not your only option. Once the base is made, you could also add shrimp, chicken, corn, potatoes, crushed tortilla chips, leftover rice, and/or other salsas, in whatever combination calls out to you.

• •

2 dried ancho chiles, stemmed and seeded (may substitute guajillo or New Mexico chiles)
½ pound dried black beans (1 heaping cup)
2 tablespoons extra-virgin olive oil
1 carrot, peeled and cut into ½-inch cubes
1 celery stalk, cut into ½-inch cubes
2 shallot lobes or ½ small onion, cut into ½-inch cubes

1 plump clove garlic, chopped
Pinch of ground cinnamon
Pinch of ground allspice
½ teaspoon kosher or coarse sea salt, plus more as needed

Tear, break, or use scissors to cut the anchos into small strips or pieces. Combine them with the beans in a large bowl and add enough water to cover by 1 inch. Let soak for at least 6 hours or overnight.

Pour the oil into a 3-quart saucepan over medium heat. When the oil starts to shimmer, add the carrot, celery, shallots, garlic, cinnamon, and allspice. Reduce the heat to medium-low, cover, and cook the vegetables slowly until they start to become tender, about 10 minutes.

Add the beans, chiles, their soaking liquid, and enough water to cover the beans by 1 inch. Increase the heat to high to bring the contents to a boil. Then decrease the heat to low so that the liquid is at a bare simmer.

Cover and gently cook until the beans are very tender, 1 to 2 hours, depending on the age of the beans. Add the salt, cook for a few more minutes, then let cool for 10 to 15 minutes.

Use a handheld immersion blender to puree the soup, then taste and adjust the salt if needed. (Alternatively, you can puree it in a blender or food processor. If you are using a blender, be sure to remove the center cap on the lid and cover with a dish towel to let steam escape, and work in small batches to avoid splattering the soup.)

Divide it into 4 portions and use immediately, refrigerate for up to 1 week, or freeze in small containers or heavy-duty freezer-safe resealable plastic bags, pressing as much air out of the bag as possible before sealing. It will keep frozen for several months.

BLACK BEAN TORTILLA SOUP
WITH SHRIMP AND CORN

This is like a taco in soup form. It is not a traditional tortilla soup, but a black bean backdrop for a double or triple hit of corn (stock, tortillas, and fresh kernels), plus just-cooked shrimp. Like a taco, it's hearty and satisfying without being fussy, and once you have the black bean soup base (page 52) ready and waiting, it's a snap to put together.

1 to 1½ cups Spicy Black Bean Soup Base (page 52), defrosted if frozen
Up to ½ cup Corn Broth (page 3), water, or chicken or vegetable stock (optional)
Kosher or sea salt
2 tablespoons extra-virgin olive oil
1 jalapeño chile
2 corn tortillas, preferably homemade (page 84)

Kernels from 1 ear fresh corn (about ¾ cup)
3 ounces very small shrimp, peeled, deveined, and cut in half lengthwise
8 small cherry tomatoes, quartered, or 2 plum tomatoes, cut into ½-inch pieces
½ lime
2 tablespoons sour cream or crème fraîche
1 tablespoon finely chopped fresh cilantro leaves

In a small saucepan over medium heat, warm the soup base. Whisk in enough corn broth to reach your desired consistency. Cook for a few minutes to heat the soup through. Taste and add more salt if desired. Decrease the heat to low, cover, and keep it hot while you make the topping.

Pour the oil into a medium skillet over medium heat. Remove the stem from the jalapeño and scrape out the ribs and seeds, reserving the seeds. Finely chop the chile and add it to the skillet. Roll the tortillas, thinly slice them, and cut the slivers in half. Add to the skillet and sauté until the tortillas are crisp, 3 to 4 minutes. Use a slotted spoon to transfer the tortillas and chile to a serving bowl.

Add the corn, shrimp, and tomatoes to the skillet. Season with salt and sauté just until the shrimp turn opaque and the corn turns bright yellow, 1 to 2 minutes.

Transfer the corn mixture to the serving bowl and pour in the black bean soup base. Squeeze the lime half onto the soup, spoon the sour cream on top, sprinkle with the cilantro, and eat.

BLACK BEAN SOUP WITH SEARED SCALLOPS AND GREEN SALSA

. . . .

Scallops are a solo cook's friend because, like shrimp, they come in easy-to-manage amounts, cook quickly, and take well to all sorts of preparations. Here, they help bulk up black bean soup into a meal. Look for "dry-packed" scallops, which are shipped without the extra water and additives that dull the flavor of wet-packed scallops, making them sweeter and easier to get a nice crust on. If you can find them, you don't need to rinse and pat them dry.

. . . .

1 to 1½ cups Spicy Black Bean Soup Base (page 52), defrosted if frozen
Up to ½ cup water or chicken or vegetable stock (optional)
½ to 1 serrano or jalapeño chile
¼ barely ripe avocado, peeled, pitted, and cut into ½-inch cubes
1 small tomatillo, husk removed, rinsed, and cut into ½-inch slices

1 very small shallot lobe, finely chopped
Leaves from 5 or 6 sprigs cilantro (about 1 tablespoon), finely chopped
Finely grated zest of 1 lime
Juice of ½ lime
1 teaspoon agave nectar or honey
3 large sea scallops (about 3 ounces)
Kosher or sea salt
1 tablespoon peanut or vegetable oil

In a small saucepan over medium heat, warm the soup base, then whisk in enough water to reach your desired consistency. Cook for a few minutes to heat the soup through, then decrease the heat to low, cover, and keep it hot while you make the topping.

Remove the stem from the serrano and scrape out the ribs and seeds, reserving the seeds. Finely chop half the serrano, then transfer it to a small bowl. Add the avocado, tomatillo, shallot, cilantro, lime zest and juice, and agave nectar; stir to combine. Taste, and if you want the salsa spicier, add some of the serrano seeds and/or the other half of the serrano, finely chopped.

Remove the large side muscles from the scallops. Then, unless they're dry-packed scallops, rinse them and thoroughly pat dry. Season the scallops with salt on each side.

Pour the oil into a medium skillet over medium-high heat. When it starts to shimmer, add the scallops, making sure they aren't touching each other. Sear until they have a ¼-inch-deep golden crust, 1 to 2 minutes. Turn them over and sear on the other side for another minute or so. They should still be slightly springy to the touch, and you should be able to tell on the sides that the middle is still slightly translucent. Transfer them to a plate.

Ladle the soup into a wide, shallow bowl, top with the salsa and then the scallops, and eat.

STEWED CAULIFLOWER, BUTTERNUT SQUASH, AND TOMATOES

Makes 6 to 7 cups

· ·

One of the smartest things you can do when cooking for one is make large quantities of pasta sauce to freeze and then defrost and adapt into quick weeknight meals. Such sauces can go well beyond a simple marinara. When I asked the queen of Italian cooking in America, Lidia Bastianich, for her favorite approaches to such a thing, she quickly came to me with this hearty vegetable stew that can do triple, quadruple, even quintuple duty: Use a cup of it to dress pasta, of course, but also spoon it onto charred bread for bruschetta, use it as a base on which to nestle grilled fish or chicken, or try one of the companion recipes: Baked Egg in Fall Vegetables (page 33) or Fall Vegetable Soup with White Beans (page 58). I couldn't resist putting my stamp on this recipe: I did what I do with many tomato sauces and splashed in some fish sauce to deepen the flavor.

· ·

½ cup extra-virgin olive oil

3 plump cloves garlic, thinly sliced

1 onion, thinly sliced

1 small (1½-pound) butternut squash, peeled, seeded, and cut into ½-inch cubes (about 3 cups)

1 (1-pound) cauliflower, cored and cut into 1-inch florets (about 3 cups)

¼ cup small capers, drained

Coarse sea salt or kosher salt

½ teaspoon red pepper flakes, or more to taste

1 (28-ounce) can Italian plum tomatoes and their juices, preferably San Marzano, crushed by hand

1 cup water

2 teaspoons Asian fish sauce, or more to taste

Pour the olive oil into a large saucepan set over medium-high heat. When the oil starts to shimmer, scatter in the sliced garlic and let it start sizzling. Stir in the onion slices and cook until wilted, about 2 minutes. Add the squash and cauliflower pieces, capers, 1 teaspoon salt, and the red pepper flakes and use tongs to toss it all together.

Pour in the crushed tomatoes and their juices. Slosh the water into the can and add; stir well and cover. When the tomato juices are boiling, decrease the heat to medium-low or low so that the mixture is gently bubbling. Cook, covered, until the vegetables

are tender, 30 to 40 minutes. Uncover, increase the heat to medium-high, and continue cooking until the stew is reduced and thickened to a good pasta-sauce consistency, about 5 minutes. Add the fish sauce, taste, and add more fish sauce and salt if desired.

Eat a cup or two as a vegetarian main course and refrigerate the leftovers in an airtight container for up to 2 weeks, or freeze it in cup-size portions for several months.

WARM SPINACH SALAD
WITH **SHIITAKES, CORN,** AND **BACON**

I never liked raw spinach that much until I started eating it from my sister's huge garden in southern Maine, where she and her husband grow almost everything they eat—a year-round endeavor, thanks to lots of canning, freezing, and the smart use of greenhouses and the like. She even brought me spinach seeds so I could start growing it in my own community garden. My garden is a tiny fraction of the size of hers, but the spinach comes out of it just as tender and sweet. This recipe barely wilts the spinach, so it still has that fresh flavor, but helps compensate for the sturdier texture of supermarket spinach, if that's what you need to use, by softening it slightly. If you have tender garden-fresh spinach, you can feel free to let the topping cool before adding it to the spinach for a cold salad instead.

3 cups packed baby spinach leaves (about
   3 ounces), tough stems discarded
1 tablespoon extra-virgin olive oil
1 slice bacon, cut into ½-inch pieces
4 ounces large shiitake mushrooms, tough stems
   removed, caps cut into ½-inch slices

Kernels from 1 ear fresh corn
1 to 2 tablespoons sherry vinegar
Kosher or sea salt
Freshly ground black pepper

Put the spinach leaves in a serving bowl.

Line a plate with paper towels. Pour the oil into a medium skillet over medium heat. When the oil starts to shimmer, add the bacon. Sauté until the bacon is crispy, 2 to 3 minutes. Use a slotted spoon to transfer it to the paper towel–lined plate, leaving as much oil in the pan as possible.

Add the shiitakes to the skillet and cook just until they exude their liquid, 2 to 3 minutes. Add the corn and cook until it turns bright yellow, 2 to 3 minutes.

Stir in 1 tablespoon of the vinegar. Taste and add more vinegar if desired, plus salt and a generous amount of black pepper.

Pour the hot mushroom and corn mixture over the spinach in the serving bowl and toss to combine thoroughly. Sprinkle the bacon pieces on top, and eat.

FALL VEGETABLE SOUP
WITH **WHITE BEANS**

This is a recipe payoff from having made the Stewed Cauliflower, Butternut Squash, and Tomatoes (page 55), beefed up with the addition of white beans, crunchy croutons, fresh thyme, and cheese. The soup is a beautiful orange color and tastes of cream, even though it has no such thing in it.

1 slice sourdough or other rustic bread, cut into
½-inch cubes
1 teaspoon extra-virgin olive oil
1 cup Stewed Cauliflower, Butternut Squash,
and Tomatoes (page 55)
¾ cup vegetable stock or water, plus more if
needed

½ cup cooked white beans, preferably homemade
(page 47), drained and rinsed
Leaves from 3 or 4 sprigs thyme
Kosher or sea salt
Freshly ground black pepper
2 tablespoons freshly grated Parmigiano-Reggiano
cheese

Preheat the oven to 425°F.

Put the bread cubes on a small baking sheet, drizzle with the oil, and toss to coat. Arrange in a single layer and toast in the oven for 5 to 6 minutes, until very crisp and golden brown, watching closely to avoid burning them. Use tongs to turn over the bread cubes and toast for another 5 to 6 minutes to create evenly browned croutons. Remove from the oven.

Combine the stewed vegetables and stock in a small saucepan over medium heat. Cook until hot, about 5 minutes.

Add the white beans and cook for a few minutes until heated through. Add more water if you want a thinner texture. Stir in the thyme. Taste and add salt and pepper, if desired.

Pour the hot soup into a bowl, add the croutons, sprinkle with the cheese, and eat.

CHAPTER 4
MEAT, POULTRY, AND SEAFOOD

The Texas boy in me, I'm afraid, would have a tough time ever giving up meat altogether. My connection to it is just plain hardwired: When I gnaw on baby-back ribs or pick at the carcass of a chicken, I'm reminded of the fact that we've evolved to be carnivores. Otherwise, why would it satisfy me on such a primal level? Of course, none of that is to say that I fault anyone for going without. To each, his own dinner.

My solo-cooking approach to animal protein boils down to this: Seek out easily portion-controlled, leaner cuts for quick weeknight dinners, but don't shy away from bigger, longer-cooking pieces to make when time allows. The key to the second idea, though, is to have a plan for what to do with all that meat: Divide it up, refrigerate or freeze it, and use it in recipes that may bear little resemblance to the original one. That avoids the boy-am-I-sick-of-eating-this-for-the-third-day syndrome.

DEEP IN THE HEART OF TEXAS, WE BREAD STEAK

I've always told people that chicken-fried steak, one of the iconic dishes of Texas, was the first thing I learned how to make, at age eight or nine, even though that's not entirely true. Mashed potatoes and whipped cream came slightly earlier; I had a thing for my mother's stand mixer. But those were mere accompaniments—a side dish, a garnish.

Anyone who has ever eaten chicken-fried steak knows that it's nothing if not a meal: a crisp, tender-but-chewy mess of meat drowning in rich, peppery cream gravy. When those mashed potatoes I had mastered took their place on the plate, too, then we were more than set. Save the diet food for another day, or another state.

My teacher was my stepfather, Vernon Lee Jones, from the little West Texas town of Miles, about 20 minutes from the relative metropolis of San Angelo, where we lived. Tall and lean, Vern's a man of few words (think of Clint Eastwood's character in *The Bridges of Madison County*). In my memory, we conducted this lesson largely in silence. But what is there to say, really, that can't be shown? Pound a piece of round steak with a spiked mallet, dredge it in seasoned flour, get some oil real hot in a cast-iron skillet, pan-fry the steak on both sides until golden brown. Pour out most of the oil; add flour and pepper and milk or cream, whisk, scrape, let thicken, and serve.

Not until I got to Austin for college did I realize there were other ways to make chicken-fried steak. In the 1980s, the dish was having a moment in such restaurants as the famous comfort-food palace Threadgill's and the retro-hip Good Eats Cafe. At those places, the breading was flakier and more distinct than Vern's, probably because the cooks were dipping the steaks in egg before flouring them. Not bad, just different.

At Good Eats, in fact, one of the most popular dishes was chicken-fried chicken, made with boneless breasts rather than steak. Think about that name: It wasn't just fried chicken, it was chicken that was fried like chicken-fried steak, which was in turn fried . . . like chicken. Perhaps only a Texan could appreciate the distinction.

I haven't lived in Texas for twenty years now, so my experiences with chicken-fried steak have been few and far between and largely of my own making. That is, until a few years ago, when the Smithsonian decided to feature Texas (along with Bhutan and NASA) at its annual Folklife Festival, which seems to always occur the hottest week of Washington's summer. Among the recipes in the arsenal of things demonstrated on the Mall that year was good old chicken-fried steak.

This recipe came with an official-sounding story of origin, one that ran somewhat counter to what I had come to believe: that chicken-fried steak must be related to schnitzel, brought by the Germans who emigrated to the Texas Hill Country. The story tells of Jimmy Don Perkins, a short-order cook at a cafe in Lamesa (even farther west than San Angelo), who on one fateful day in 1911 wrongly assumed that a waitress's ticket for two orders ("chicken, fried steak") was for only one. He had never heard of it, but figured the only way to make it was to cook the steak like fried chicken. So that's what he did.

The venerable Texas food authority Robb Walsh, in what may be the definitive treatise on chicken-fried steak in a 2007 article for the *Houston Press*, broke down the dish into three distinct versions, theorizing that each may have a separate heritage. The East Texas one, dipped in egg and then flour, is probably connected to Southern fried chicken. The Central Texas version, sometimes using bread crumbs in the mixture, probably comes from those German immigrants. And the eggless West Texas version I learned to make is probably more closely related to what the cowboys called pan-fried steak.

But there are exceptions to everything. The citified versions I tasted in Austin didn't use bread crumbs. Neither does the Smithsonian recipe, provided by Tom Nall of Burnet, also in Central Texas. What's more, Nall uses Bisquick for a final coat.

As a purist, my hackles were raised, but when I tested his recipe, I have to say, I loved it. The breading was extra flaky, no doubt from the baking soda in the Bisquick, and the gravy was perfectly spiced, thanks to a few dashes of Tabasco and a pinch of sugar. It took me back to Texas, if not quite all the way to my childhood home in San Angelo, at least to Threadgill's in Austin.

I made it for a friend. He was enthusiastic about the steak and the breading but less so about the characteristically thick gravy. "It's so heavy and peppery," he said, "and it fights with the beef. Can you rework the recipe to make it thinner, maybe a little lighter?"

He's Canadian, so I should have cut him some slack. Instead, I told him yes, I most certainly can make the gravy thinner or lighter, but I won't. Not without the approval of Vernon Lee Jones of Miles, Texas, and I already know what he would say. Or what he wouldn't.

PAN-FRIED SIRLOIN WITH SMASHED POTATOES AND ANCHOVY SAUCE

Despite all my big Texas talk, the truth is, I don't make classic chicken-fried steak for myself. Between the prep work and the calorie count, it's just not practical. Instead, I make something that requires no pounding, no dredging in egg and flour, no inch of oil in the pan. It's inspired by my favorite steaks growing up: those at Margaret Heinen's Western Sky, where the cooks would rub crushed garlic into the steaks, very lightly dredge them in flour, and grill them over wood. The light coating was positively delectable. I pan-fry my steak, pair it with boiled and smashed new potatoes, and finish them both with a quick sauce of anchovies, butter, and parsley. I don't call this chicken-fried, for obvious reasons, but it tastes like Texas just the same.

2 or 3 small new potatoes (about 3 ounces total), scrubbed
1 (4-ounce) boneless sirloin steak, preferably no more than ½ inch thick, trimmed of excess fat
1 plump clove garlic
Kosher or sea salt
Freshly ground black pepper

1 tablespoon all-purpose flour
2 tablespoons extra-virgin olive oil
1 anchovy fillet, finely chopped
1 tablespoon unsalted butter
Juice of ½ lemon
1 tablespoon finely chopped fresh parsley leaves

Bring a 2-quart saucepan of water to a boil. Add the potatoes and cook until very tender when poked with a skewer or fork, 15 to 18 minutes, depending on their size. Drain and let cool.

While the potatoes are cooking, pat dry the steak with paper towels. If it is much thicker than ½ inch, press it with your palms to flatten it slightly.

Finely chop the garlic, sprinkle ½ teaspoon of salt onto it on your cutting board, and chop some more, smearing it with the side of your knife to make a paste. Rub the garlic paste into the steak on both sides. Generously season the steak with black pepper. Sprinkle the flour all over the steak, spreading the flour on lightly with your fingers. Gently shake off the excess flour.

Pour the olive oil into a medium cast-iron skillet over medium heat. When the oil is shimmering, lay the steak in the pan and let it cook until the coating on the bottom turns golden brown, about 2 minutes. Turn the steak over and cook on the other side for

another minute or so, for a medium-rare to medium steak. Transfer the steak to a plate and loosely cover it with aluminum foil to keep warm.

Pour off all but a teaspoon or so of the oil from the skillet and return it to medium heat.

When the potatoes are cool enough to handle, transfer them to your countertop and use a spatula or the side of a cook's knife and your palm to gently flatten them. Season lightly with salt, then use a spatula to transfer them to the skillet. Cook until golden brown, 2 to 3 minutes per side. (It's okay if they break up a little in the pan.) Transfer the potatoes to the plate with the steak.

Add the anchovy to the skillet, still over medium heat. Add the butter and cook until it melts and foams. Scrape up any browned bits in the pan, then stir in the lemon juice and parsley.

Pour the sauce over the steak and potatoes, and eat.

TEXAS BOWL O' RED

Makes 2 servings

My brother Michael once told me the two questions I should ask anyone who claims to make real (i.e., Texas-style) chili. Question one: What kind of beans do you put in it? Question two: What kind of tomatoes do you use? Both are trick questions, of course, because the answer to both is none. There are no beans and no tomatoes in real Texas chili. The full name is "chili con carne," and that's what it means: chile peppers with meat, and very little else. When done right, it's a beautiful thing. With only one kind of chile and at least 6 hours of simmering, it's got the round flavors and slow-burning heat that define a "bowl o' red." If you want something hotter, add up to 1 teaspoon of cayenne pepper, or to taste. I usually make at least two servings, because after eating the first one (with saltines, grated Cheddar cheese, chopped onions, and, okay, even pinto beans as long as they're on the side), I love the second serving on a hot dog or burger, or as part of enchiladas (page 64).

3 dried ancho chiles
2 cups dark beer, beef stock, or water, plus more
  as needed
1 tablespoon vegetable oil
1 pound beef stew meat or chuck roast (trimmed of
  excess fat), cut into ½-inch pieces (not ground)
Kosher or sea salt
Freshly ground black pepper

2 cloves garlic, finely chopped
2 large shallot lobes, finely chopped
2 tablespoons dried oregano (preferably Mexican)
1 tablespoon ground cumin
1 teaspoon pimenton (smoked Spanish paprika)
Ground cayenne pepper (optional)
1 to 2 ounces Cheddar cheese, grated
Saltine crackers

Cut or tear apart the ancho chiles, discarding the seeds and stems. Toss them into a dry skillet over medium heat and toast for 5 minutes, just until fragrant, without allowing them to char. Transfer them to a blender, pour in ½ cup of the beer, and blend until smooth.

Heat the oil in a small Dutch oven over medium-high heat until it shimmers. Season the beef generously with salt and pepper. When the oil shimmers, add just enough meat to the pot to avoid overcrowding. Cook in batches, stirring frequently, until the beef starts to brown, 3 to 4 minutes per batch.

Return all the meat to the pot, add the garlic and half the chopped shallots, and cook for a few minutes, stirring constantly, until the beef is browned all over and the garlic and shallots are soft. Stir in the oregano, cumin, pimenton, and ancho puree. Add enough of the remaining 1½ cups beer to cover the meat by 1 inch.

Bring to a boil, decrease the heat to low so that the mixture is at a bare simmer, and cover. Cook for 6 hours, stirring occasionally if desired. Uncover and use a spatula to mash and break up the meat. Cook, uncovered, for another hour or two, until the chili has become quite thick and the meat has almost melted into the liquid. Taste and adjust the seasoning with salt and cayenne pepper.

Spoon half the chili into a bowl, sprinkle with the remaining chopped shallots and the cheese, and eat with saltines. Refrigerate the remaining half in an airtight container for up to 1 week, or freeze for several months.

Note: This recipe doubles easily, if you'd like more of a payoff for your time. You can also make this in a small slow cooker. Cook on Low for 6 to 8 hours, then uncover, turn to High, and cook for another hour to thicken the chili.

CHILI CHEESE ENCHILADAS

Makes 1 or 2 servings

. . . .

One of Austin's oldest restaurants is the venerable Texas Chili Parlor; its motto is "E Pluribus Chili," and its signature dish comes in three levels of heat: X, XX, and XXX. The X is fantastic: plenty spicy, but you can still taste the other flavors. To my taste, XX is just slightly over the line between hot and too hot. And the XXX—well, let's just say they make you sign a waiver before you can order it, and I never have. Besides the basic chili, my favorite item on the menu is the cheese enchiladas topped with the chili. They call them Frieda's Enchiladas, and in all the years I went there, I never asked who Frieda was. I guess my mouth was always full, on fire, or both. This is my interpretation based on countless samplings. Now, this recipe may make enough for two servings, depending on your appetite and whether you eat beans and rice on the side, but I confess: I'm usually a four-enchilada man, meaning I have to commit to some extra time at the gym, but it's worth it.

. . . .

4 corn tortillas, preferably homemade (page 84)
Cooking oil spray or extra-virgin olive oil
1 cup shredded Cheddar cheese

1 large shallot, finely chopped
1 cup Texas Bowl o' Red (page 63)

Preheat the oven to 400°F.

Heat a small skillet set over medium heat, and soften the tortillas by spraying each on both sides with cooking oil spray or brushing them with olive oil, and then heating them in the skillet, one at a time, for a minute or two on each side. Transfer them to a plate and cover with a paper towel. Spray a small baking dish or pie plate with cooking oil spray or brush with more olive oil.

To roll the enchiladas, set a tortilla on your work surface and put about 3 tablespoons of cheese and 1 teaspoon of shallots about an inch or two from the edge closest to you. Roll the tortilla around the filling. Place the filled tortilla in the baking dish, seam side down. Fill the remaining tortillas and fit into the prepared baking dish. Pour the chili on top of the enchiladas and sprinkle the remaining 4 tablespoons cheese and shallots on top.

Bake for about 15 minutes, or until the cheese is melted and the chili is bubbling. Transfer to a plate, and eat.

SPICY GLAZED MINI MEATLOAF

Makes 4 servings

. . . .

I loosely based this recipe on one in Lynn Alley's *The Gourmet Toaster Oven*, and it works well in that device, something that single cooks should consider adding to their countertops to help save energy when making small quantities. But it also bakes just fine in a regular oven. This recipe makes four small meatloaves; the idea is that you freeze three of them and bake one at a time. But the meat can also be baked in a loaf pan and sliced into portions after baking. (You'll have to bake it a bit longer to get the internal temperature up to 160°F.) The recipe is also flexible flavor-wise: If you don't have some of the Blackened Salsa (page 16) in your fridge, just use a store-bought salsa, and choose mild to hot depending on your preference. Eat this with roasted, mashed, or scalloped potatoes (or root vegetables) and a crisp green salad.

. . . .

1 pound lean ground beef
½ cup dried bread crumbs
1 egg, lightly beaten
⅓ cup Blackened Salsa (page 16) or salsa of your choice
¼ cup finely chopped fresh flat-leaf parsley leaves

2 teaspoons Dijon mustard
1 teaspoon kosher or coarse sea salt
1 tablespoon freshly ground black pepper
3 tablespoons grape or apple jelly
½ teaspoon hot pepper sauce, such as Tabasco

Preheat the oven to 350°F. Use nonstick cooking oil spray to lightly grease the insides of four (4- to 5-ounce) ramekins.

Combine the beef, bread crumbs, egg, salsa, parsley, mustard, salt, and pepper in a large bowl and mix until well incorporated. Divide the meat mixture into 4 equal portions; form each into a ball, then lightly press them into the ramekins, leaving each with a domed top.

Combine the jelly and hot pepper sauce in a microwave-safe container. Microwave on High for about 30 seconds to soften the jelly. Whisk to form a glaze, then use a spoon to drizzle it on top of each meatloaf; there may be some leftover glaze,

which can be used to drizzle or brush on the baked meatloaf. Wrap 3 of the ramekins tightly in plastic wrap for freezing.

Bake the remaining meatloaf for about 20 minutes, or until it is nicely browned on top and its interior temperature registers at least 160°F on an instant-read thermometer. Let cool slightly, then unmold, and place on a plate, glazed side up. If desired, drizzle or brush the meatloaf with any remaining glaze before eating.

Note: The unbaked meatloaves freeze well for up to 1 month; let defrost in the refrigerator before baking.

YUCATAN-STYLE SLOW-ROASTED PORK

Makes 4 to 5 cups, or 6 to 8 servings

. . . .

Of all the recipes in the cookbook I cowrote with Boston chef Andy Husbands, *The Fearless Chef*, the one for slow-roasted pork is the one I'm asked for the most. A new round of requests came after my friend Josh and I made it for my own birthday party a few years ago in Washington. We served it simply, with salsa, sour cream, and tortillas on the side, but trust me, this meat can go into all sorts of recipes, such as in Cochinita Pibil Tacos (page 95), Faux-lognese with Pappardelle (page 140), and Pulled Pork Sandwich with Green Mango Slaw (page 121). I've simplified this recipe a little from Andy's original version, cutting out a 24-hour marinating step, replacing the traditional banana leaves with good old aluminum foil, and using one of my favorite smoke stand-ins, Spanish pimenton (smoked Spanish paprika), instead of oregano. The pork is spicy and deeply flavored and colored, thanks in no small part to the large quantity of annatto seeds (also called achiote) that goes into the paste. These little brick-colored pebbles are worth seeking out at good Latin markets or online through such sources as Penzeys.com.

. . . .

3 tablespoons annatto seeds

3 tablespoons whole black peppercorns

1 tablespoon toasted cumin seeds

¾ cup peeled garlic cloves

¾ cup lightly packed fresh cilantro leaves and stems

1½ tablespoons kosher or coarse sea salt

1 seedless orange, peeled and cut into large chunks

¼ cup beer of any type

2 teaspoons red pepper flakes

1 teaspoon ground allspice

1 teaspoon pimenton (smoked Spanish paprika)

1 teaspoon ground ancho chile

3 pounds fresh pork shoulder (Boston butt or picnic shoulder)

Preheat the oven to 275°F.

Using a spice grinder (such as a coffee grinder reserved for spices), grind the annatto seeds, peppercorns, and cumin seeds to a fine powder.

In the bowl of a food processor, combine the garlic cloves, cilantro, and salt and process until finely chopped. Add the orange, beer, red pepper flakes, allspice, pimenton, ground ancho, and the ground annatto mixture and process until a fairly smooth paste forms.

Lay a 2-foot sheet of aluminum foil on your work surface. Set the pork in the middle of it. Spread the spicy paste over the pork, coating it on all sides,

then tightly roll up the pork inside the foil, tucking in the sides as you go, as if you're making a burrito. Use another long strip of foil to create another layer, being sure to seal the pork tightly inside the foil. Place the pork packet in a roasting pan, fill it with water to come a couple of inches up the side of the foil-wrapped pork, then use another piece of aluminum foil to cover and seal the whole pan.

Roast the pork until you can feel it falling apart inside its package if you push on it, and a skewer inserted through the top of the foil and into the meat encounters no resistance, 4 to 5 hours. (If you're not sure, err on the side of longer cooking; you really can't overcook this.)

Remove the roast in its foil from the pan, transfer to a platter, and let it cool for at least 30 minutes before slashing open the foil. Discard any large pieces of fat, and use two forks to shred the meat. Combine the meat with enough of the sauce created from the spices and pan drippings so that it is very juicy but not swimming, reserving the rest of this sauce for other uses, such as spooning onto pan-fried pork chops or adding extra moisture to the Pulled Pork Sandwich with Green Mango Slaw (page 121).

Eat one serving of the meat however you like (with tortillas, Citrus-Pickled Onions, page 19, and sour cream is a good bet) while letting the rest cool to room temperature. Refrigerate the leftovers for up to 1 week or divide into 4 to 6 portions, seal in heavy-duty plastic freezer bags, removing as much air as possible, and freeze for up to 6 months.

PORK CHOP WITH APPLES AND BRUSSELS SPROUTS

Apples, pork, and cabbage would seem best for fall, but I confess to making this dish anytime I get a hankering for a pork chop and see Brussels sprouts in the market. The tart apple and spicy ginger give it an appealing lightness. I like to use Brussels sprouts for single-serving dishes for an obvious reason: There's less possible waste than with a big head of cabbage.

1 (4-ounce) bone-in pork chop, preferably no more than ½ inch thick
Kosher or sea salt
Freshly ground black pepper
½ Granny Smith apple
3 or 4 Brussels sprouts
1 tablespoon extra-virgin olive oil

1 shallot lobe, thinly sliced
1-inch piece fresh ginger, peeled and finely chopped
1 tablespoon mirin (Japanese cooking wine) or sherry
1 teaspoon unseasoned rice vinegar

Pat dry the pork chop with a paper towel and season generously with salt and pepper on both sides. Cut the apple in half, core, and cut it into 8 wedges. Thinly slice the wedges crosswise. Remove and discard the tough outer layer of leaves from the Brussels sprouts, cut them in halves, and cut out and discard the tough core. Thinly slice lengthwise.

Pour the oil into a large, cold cast-iron skillet, press the pork chop into the cold pan, and turn it to medium heat. When you hear the pork chop start to sizzle, after about 1 or 2 minutes, scatter the shallot and ginger around it. Stir the shallot and ginger occasionally to keep them from burning, but leave

the pork chop undisturbed, cooking until very lightly browned on one side, about 2 to 3 minutes. Turn the chop over, add the apple and Brussels sprouts to the pan, and season them lightly with salt. Stir to combine the apples and sprouts with the shallot and ginger, while leaving the pork undisturbed, and sprinkle the mirin and rice vinegar over the vegetables. Decrease the heat to medium-low, cover the pan and cook until the pork has just barely reached 140°F when tested with an instant-read thermometer and the sprouts have wilted, 3 to 4 minutes.

Transfer the pork to a serving plate and let it rest for a few minutes. Spoon the apple mixture on top, and eat.

FIRST, KILL YOUR CHICKEN

Talk about executing a recipe.

There I knelt, hatchet in one hand and a living, breathing chicken in the other. I held it by its feet, and its head lay across the chopping block. It didn't cluck, didn't flap. It was calm—certainly calmer than I. My heart thumped; my stomach somersaulted into nausea. As I raised the hatchet, I thought, "I can't do this. I can't kill this chicken."

Then I took another breath.

And I remembered that as anxious as I was, this situation was of my own doing. I had asked to slaughter this animal—and only partly so that I would get the rare chance to write "like a chicken with its head cut off," and mean it.

When my sister Rebekah and her fiancé announced almost ten years ago that they were going to start raising chickens at their home in North Berwick, Maine—for both eggs and meat—I immediately knew I wanted in.

My reasons? This was years before Michael Pollan immortalized the ideas in *The Omnivore's Dilemma*, but I thought that I should be capable of killing a chicken, as a culinary student at the time and as a meat eater who didn't want to be hypocritical. Plus, like so many before and since, I had become increasingly distrustful of the food industry; I wanted to know more about the origins of the food going into my body.

I also knew the feat would be a challenge because I've never been much of a hunter. My stepfather took me once when I was a kid in West Texas, and while I was a pretty good shot (what Texas boy isn't?), I couldn't bring myself to aim at a living thing and pull the trigger. I also found hunting exceedingly boring, much the way I felt about fishing.

My resistance to killing occurred before I heard Diane Sawyer use the term "fecal soup" on *20/20* some years earlier, in a show on chicken-processing plants, which drove me to experiment with vegetarianism (unsuccessfully). It was before I started my studies at the Cambridge School of Culinary Arts, where an instructor delivered a lecture on the same subject and had us all turning green in our seats. It was before my sister moved from Boston to Maine, where her back-to-the-land life echoed her hippie days of make-your-own everything.

continued

When I mentioned my plans for chicken execution, most people quickly recalled a grandmother or great-aunt who could do the deed with a simple flick of the wrist—or wrists, with a bird in each hand.

In the same breath, though, they said, "Not me. Somebody else can do it. I don't want to know about it. Give me the plastic-wrapped package in the store."

A place like Mayflower Poultry near Boston, then, with its famous "Live Poultry, Fresh Killed" sign, made such folks gulp. More and more, it makes me hungry. I haven't seen the whole operation, but the chickens are tasty, the storefront is nice and clean, and in one spotless room visible from the street, I've seen workers dressed in all white, wearing plastic gloves as they cut up chickens.

A far cry from what Diane Sawyer saw. She was talking about one of the processing-plant baths, in which chickens whose intestines had been accidentally ruptured by machinery were "washed" in the same water with cleaner ones—probably infecting them all with salmonella. (If you don't own a meat thermometer, buy one. Salmonella dies at 165°F.)

These days, of course, you can get some high-quality chickens in stores more accessible than Mayflower Poultry. Farmers' markets sell delicious birds raised with access to the outdoors and with feeds free of hormones and other additives. Natural-food stores carry Bell and Evans and other brands that also produce free-range birds fed on natural diets. I like to believe that such companies' production methods are more sanitary than at the giant firms Sawyer was talking about.

But my sister and her fiancé, Peter, decided they wanted more control than merely driving 45 minutes to a fancy market. I didn't blame them, and I wanted to join them, at least for a weekend here and there. So when my sister asked me what I wanted for my birthday, I said, "A chicken. One of yours. But only if you let me kill it."

So on my birthday, behind a shed at Rebekah and Peter's house, I took the situation into my own hands. And despite the nausea, the second thoughts, and the pounding heart, I took a deep breath and let the hatchet fall. The chicken went from calm to frantic, from alive to dead, from lying on the chopping block to running around—indeed, like a chicken with its head cut off. Exactly.

After the quick plucking and cleaning (I took extra care to eviscerate without puncturing the intestines), we let the meat rest in the fridge. Then we went outside and foraged in the garden, slicing Brussels sprouts right off the stalk, kneeling to slash rainbow chard leaves at the stem, and reaching through leaves to pull up smooth butternut squash. For the outdoor table, we picked flowers and Concord grapes, and lit the scene with candles made from the wax from the beehive out back.

We stuffed the bird with lemon and garlic and roasted it alongside an identically prepared Whole Foods chicken, for comparison. We tossed the Brussels sprouts and chard in butter and Parmigiano-Reggiano cheese; roasted potatoes and tomatoes in olive oil, the former doused in rosemary and the latter in garlic; and baked the squash in a mint vinaigrette. This birthday dinner approached the magical. When I brought out the chocolate-chestnut cake I had started in Boston and finished in Maine, the starlit table was overflowing with family and friends, who were drinking sangria and pulling on sweaters as the almost-fall chill hit the air.

How was the chicken? Well, to be honest, it was tougher than the velvety store-bought version—probably the beginnings of rigor mortis, which we could've avoided by letting the meat rest another day. But it was much fuller in flavor, almost as if the meat had been seasoned from the bone out.

The best part, though, was that I knew exactly how it lived, and just how it died. And that made it all the more delicious.

ROAST CHICKEN LEG WITH GREMOLATA AND SUNCHOKES

If you're like me and prefer dark meat, the easiest way to satisfy your roast-chicken urges without tackling a whole bird is to take advantage of one of my favorite cuts: the whole leg, with thigh and drumstick attached. It makes a hearty meal, and it takes well to the same kind of classic preparations a whole chicken does, including roasting with the magical trio of parsley, lemon, and garlic. If you don't have a jar of Herbed Lemon Confit (page 4) in the refrigerator, you can substitute store-bought preserved lemon or even just two fresh lemon slices (peel and pith included) plus an extra 1 teaspoon of olive oil. Feel free to roast more sunchokes and use the leftovers to toss into salads, mash like potatoes, or puree in soups.

1 whole chicken leg (thigh and drumstick attached,
    8 to 10 ounces)
Kosher or sea salt
Freshly ground black pepper
2 cloves garlic, 1 finely chopped and 1 sliced
¼ cup fresh parsley leaves, finely chopped

2 slices Herbed Lemon Confit (page 4), gently
    shaken of excess oil and finely chopped
½ pound sunchokes, scrubbed, unpeeled, and cut
    into ½-inch cubes
1 teaspoon extra-virgin olive oil
½ lemon

Preheat the oven to 450°F.

Sprinkle the chicken leg generously with salt and pepper.

In a small bowl, stir together the chopped garlic, parsley, and lemon confit to form the gremolata. Add oil from the jar of lemon confit if needed to form a paste. Use your finger to loosen the skin over the chicken thigh and drumstick, then pack the gremolata inside, reserving a tablespoon or so to rub on the outside of the skin.

Scatter the sunchokes and sliced garlic in a small cast-iron skillet. Drizzle with the olive oil, season with salt and pepper, and toss to thoroughly coat with the oil. Push to the edges of the pan and put the chicken in the middle.

Roast the chicken until the skin is browned and crisp and an instant-read thermometer inserted into the thickest part of the thigh reads at least 165°F, 20 to 30 minutes. Baste it with the oil in the pan a time or two during roasting, if desired. Remove from the oven, and let the chicken and sunchokes rest for a few minutes in the pan.

Transfer the chicken and sunchokes to the dinner plate, squeeze the lemon half over the chicken, and eat.

PINEAPPLE-JUICE-CAN HEN
AND BABY POTATOES

Roast chicken is one of my I-can't-have-it-around-or-I'll-eat-the-whole-thing addictions. After the first meal, the rest of the bird sits front and center in my refrigerator, and when the urge hits, I pull off a piece here and there until the carcass is picked clean. Anyway, that's one of the reasons I am drawn to smaller birds: guinea hens, squab, poussin. They're certainly on the high end in terms of fat and calories, but at least when I'm done, I'm done. No more temptations. When I saw ¾-pound hens at one of my favorite vendors (Eco-Friendly Farms) at the Sunday farmers' market in Washington's Dupont Circle, I had a brainstorm: Why not treat them like beer-can chicken (more colloquially known as beer-butt chicken), but with a smaller can of pineapple juice instead? I thought it was the most original thing ever, until I Googled around and saw that others had trod this ground before me, including barbecue maestro Steven Raichlen. I forged ahead, combining the pineapple with one of its natural partners—rosemary—and cooking down extra juice with lime and butter into a sweet-and-sour glaze. With roasted potatoes (babies, of course), I had a meal.

1 guinea or Cornish hen or other small bird
  (preferably no bigger than ¾ pound)
2 teaspoons unsalted butter, at room temperature
Kosher or sea salt
Freshly ground black pepper
3 sprigs rosemary

1 (6-ounce) can pineapple juice
3 very small potatoes (baby Yukon gold or red
  new), cut into ½-inch pieces
1 teaspoon extra-virgin olive oil
1 tablespoon freshly squeezed lime juice, plus
  more to taste

Preheat the oven to 425°F.

Rinse the hen under cold running water, then pat dry with paper towels. Remove the packet of giblets, if there is one, and discard or save for another use. Rub the hen with 1 teaspoon of the butter, then sprinkle generously with salt and pepper inside and out. Loosen the skin over the breasts and tuck one of the rosemary sprigs under the skin on each side.

Shake the pineapple juice well, remove the paper exterior from the can, rinse, and dry the can. Use a can opener to completely remove the top of the can. Pour half of the pineapple juice into another container and reserve for another use. (Or drink it while you cook!)

Spray the can's exterior with cooking oil spray. Set the can in the middle of a small, oven-proof skillet and set the hen on top of it, carefully working the can into the hen's cavity without spilling the juice. Scatter the potatoes around the hen, season them with salt and pepper, drizzle with the olive oil, and scatter the leaves from the remaining rosemary sprig around them.

Roast the hen for 30 to 40 minutes, until it is nicely browned, the juices run clear, and an instant-read thermometer inserted into the thickest part of the thigh reads at least 165°F. Remove from the oven, use oven mitts or tongs to remove it from the pineapple juice can, and transfer the hen to a serving plate; let it rest for about 10 minutes. If the potatoes are not fork-tender, return the potatoes to the oven to continue cooking while the hen rests.

While the hen is resting, pour the contents of the pineapple juice can into a small saucepan set over medium-high heat. Add the lime juice and remaining 1 teaspoon butter. Bring to a boil and let it bubble away until it has reduced to a syrupy glaze, about 10 minutes.

Cut the hen in half with a sharp chef's knife or poultry shears, and scatter the roasted potatoes around it. Drizzle the hen with the pineapple-lime glaze, and eat it while it's hot.

Note: If you can't find the small cans of pineapple juice (they often come in 6-packs), wash out a small can of tomato paste and pour juice into it. If you can only find larger hens, adjust the cooking time to compensate and save some as leftovers for another day.

WINE-BRAISED CHICKEN THIGHS WITH OLIVES, PRUNES, AND ALMONDS

I confess I'm not a big fan of boneless, skinless chicken breasts, which I find tasteless enough to be considered the tofu of meats (no offense, tofu lovers). Instead, for most purposes I almost always go for the thighs, with the bone in for more flavor and quicker, more even cooking. I like to leave the skin on, too; however, in a quick braise like this one, it can get too rubbery. This is a very stripped-down take on traditional Moorish flavor combinations; eat it with white or brown rice or farro (see page 143), which will soak up the complex sauce wonderfully.

1 tablespoon sliced almonds
1 teaspoon extra-virgin olive oil
1 clove garlic, thinly sliced
2 small bone-in, skinless chicken thighs (about 6 to 8 ounces total)
Kosher or sea salt

Freshly ground black pepper
6 large green olives, pitted and chopped
4 prunes, pitted and chopped
⅔ cup fruity red wine
1 tablespoon unsalted butter (optional)

Toast the almonds in a small dry skillet over medium-high heat, stirring constantly, until they are lightly browned and begin to smell toasty, 2 to 3 minutes. Watch carefully; nuts can burn quickly. Immediately transfer to a dish to cool.

Pour the oil into the skillet you used for toasting the nuts and set over medium heat. When the oil starts to shimmer, scatter the garlic slices in the pan and cook, stirring occasionally, until the garlic is tender and starts to brown, 2 to 3 minutes. Remove the garlic with a slotted spoon to a plate.

Increase the heat to medium-high. Season the chicken thighs generously with salt and pepper, set them in the pan, bone side up, and cook until they are deeply golden brown, 5 to 6 minutes. Repeat on the other side.

Return the garlic slices to the pan, along with the green olives and prunes. Pour in the red wine and immediately decrease the heat until the liquid is barely simmering. Cover the pan with a tight-fitting lid or double layer of aluminum foil. Let the chicken cook undisturbed until an instant-read thermometer inserted into its thickest part (without touching bone) reads at least 165°F, about 10 minutes.

Remove the cover and use tongs to transfer the chicken to the dinner plate. Loosely cover with foil. Increase the heat to high and let the wine sauce bubble for a few minutes until it thickens. Taste, adjust the seasoning as necessary, and add butter if you'd like a little more richness.

Pour the sauce over the chicken on the plate, top with the toasted almonds, and eat.

CORNISH HEN WITH CHERRY-HAZELNUT WINE SAUCE

When I first visited Portland, Oregon, I left with two regrets: that I didn't plan on more days (so I could eat more) in that glorious food-obsessed city, and that I didn't pack an extra duffel for all the edible stuff I wanted to carry back home. On that last point, I limited myself to dried sour cherries and dry-roasted hazelnuts. When I wasn't scarfing them out of hand, I threw them into dishes, alone but often in combination, proving the validity of the saying, "If it grows together, it goes together." For this dish, I turned the hazelnuts and dried cherries into a sauce that can be made with Mulled Wine Syrup (page 6) or Pinot Noir (another Oregon specialty) to pour over pan-fried Cornish hen. I like to cook it al mattone, which means "with a brick," a quick method that results in even cooking, a crisp skin, and moist flesh.

2 tablespoons raw hazelnuts
1 Cornish hen or other small hen (about ¾ pound)
¼ teaspoon kosher or coarse sea salt
½ teaspoon ground allspice
1 tablespoon fat-free Greek-style yogurt
1 teaspoon extra-virgin olive oil

3 tablespoons Mulled Wine Syrup (page 7) made with red wine (or substitute ½ cup Pinot Noir or other fruity red wine plus ½ teaspoon sugar, or more to taste)
2 to 3 tablespoons dried cherries, preferably unsweetened
Freshly ground black pepper

Toast the hazelnuts in a small, dry skillet over medium-high heat, stirring constantly, until they are lightly browned and begin to smell toasty, 1 to 5 minutes. Watch carefully; nuts can burn quickly. Transfer to the folds of a clean dish towel to remove the skins while the nuts are still warm, then discard the skins and let the nuts cool. Coarsely chop the nuts.

Using poultry shears or a very sharp knife, cut along each side of the hen's backbone and remove it. Turn the hen over on your cutting board, splay it out butterfly-style, and press on the breastbone to break it. Sprinkle it with salt and allspice then rub the yogurt all over it.

Heat the olive oil in a large nonstick skillet over medium-high heat until it starts to shimmer. Place the hen, meat side down, in the skillet and weight it down with a smaller skillet with a large can of tomatoes or other heavy object on top. (Or, do as I do, and use a heavy cast-iron bacon press, made for just this kind of thing.)

Let the hen cook until the yogurt has formed a dark brown crust on the meat side, 5 to 10 minutes. Lift off the weight assembly, and use tongs to turn the hen over onto the bone side. Return the weights and cook until an internal thermometer inserted into the thickest part of the thigh and the breast reads at least 165°F, another 5 to 6 minutes. Transfer to a plate and loosely cover with aluminum foil while you make the sauce.

Pour the wine syrup into the skillet and use a spatula to scrape up any browned bits from the bottom of the pan. Add the dried cherries and hazelnuts, stir to combine, and season with salt and pepper to taste. (If you're using wine instead of the syrup, pour it in, scrape up the browned bits from the pan, add the dried cherries and hazelnuts, then let the wine bubble and reduce by about half. Add the sugar to taste and continue reducing the sauce until it is thick and sticky, then season with salt and pepper to taste.)

Remove the sauce from the heat, spoon the sauce over the hen, and eat.

MAHI MAHI WITH KIWI-AVOCADO SALSA AND COCONUT RICE

· ·

When the cooking times match up, it only makes sense to cook a protein and a starch together, as in this combination of fish and rice. It's almost a one-dish meal, and I say almost because you do need to pull out a little bowl to make the spicy-sweet salsa while the pot simmers on the stovetop. This features my favorite way to make rice, an adaptation of the traditional coconut-milk rice that tastes good but is high in fat. The proliferation of coconut water as a healthful drink found in most supermarkets gave me a lighter—and, frankly, better—way to do it, and I haven't looked back. Be sure to buy juice labeled 100% coconut water, as some juice-pack brands have other flavorings you wouldn't want here, and some canned products include sugar and preservatives, defeating the purpose altogether.

· ·

1 (6-ounce) mahi mahi fillet (or substitute halibut)
Kosher or sea salt
Freshly ground black pepper
¾ cup coconut water
⅓ cup jasmine or other long-grain white rice
1 kiwi, peeled and cut into ½-inch cubes
½ ripe avocado, peeled, pitted, and cut into ½-inch cubes

1 scallion, white and green parts, cut into ¼-inch slices
½ fresh jalapeño chile, stemmed, seeded, and finely chopped (optional)
Juice of 1 lime
Leaves from 3 or 4 sprigs cilantro, chopped
½ teaspoon honey, or more to taste (optional)

Pat dry the mahi mahi with a paper towel and sprinkle with salt and pepper.

In a small skillet or saucepan fitted with a lid, combine the coconut water, rice, and ¼ teaspoon of salt over medium-high heat. Bring to a boil, then decrease the heat until the liquid is barely bubbling. Place the mahi mahi fillet on top of the rice, cover, and cook for about 15 minutes, or until all the coconut water is absorbed. Turn off the heat and let the rice and fish stand, covered, for another 5 minutes.

While the rice and fish are cooking, make the salsa. In a small bowl, stir together the kiwi, avocado, scallion, jalapeño, lime juice, and cilantro. Taste and add a touch of salt if necessary and a drizzle of honey if it's too tart.

Transfer the rice and fish to a plate, top with the salsa, and eat.

TURBOT WITH TOMATOES, WALNUTS, AND CAPERS OVER COUSCOUS

I got the idea for packing pungent combinations of toppings onto fish before it cooks from Nate Appleman's gorgeous book, *A16: Food + Wine*. I like to take it a step further and cook the fish over saffron-infused beads of Israeli couscous. This recipe is a great use for my 12-Hour Tomatoes (page 2), but if you don't already have some in your refrigerator, you can substitute three or four sun-dried tomato halves packed in oil. Eat this fish with sautéed greens or a salad.

2 tablespoons raw walnut pieces
1 (6-ounce) turbot fillet (or substitute sole or halibut)
Kosher or sea salt
Freshly ground black pepper
2 large 12-Hour Tomatoes (page 2), drained and coarsely chopped

1 teaspoon capers, drained
1 teaspoon za'atar
½ cup water
⅓ cup Israeli couscous
Pinch of saffron threads

Toast the walnut pieces in a small, dry skillet over medium-high heat, shaking the skillet frequently, until they are very fragrant and starting to brown, 3 to 4 minutes. Immediately transfer the nuts to a plate, let cool, and then coarsely chop.

Lightly season the turbot fillet with salt and pepper. Combine the tomatoes, walnuts, capers, and za'atar in a small bowl and mix well. Pack on top of the turbot fillet.

Pour the water into a small saucepan fitted with a lid over medium-high heat. Bring to a boil, decrease the heat until the water is at a bare simmer, and stir in the couscous, saffron, and a sprinkling of salt. Place the turbot fillet on top of the couscous and water, cover, and let cook until the couscous has absorbed almost all of the water and the turbot flakes easily with a fork, about 10 minutes.

Use a large spatula to carefully lift the turbot and transfer it to a plate, spoon the couscous around it, and eat.

Note: Za'atar is a tangy Middle Eastern spice blend that includes sumac and is found in Middle Eastern markets or online at Penzeys.com. If you can't find it easily, you can use a dried Italian herb mix instead, for a slightly different flavor.

GINGERY GLAZED HALIBUT
WITH CARROTS AND BABY BOK CHOY

In Buddhism, patience is more than a virtue; it's one of the "six perfections" that can lead to enlightenment. I thought about that the first several times I tried this dish, which is inspired by a technique developed by chef Eric Ripert. Ripert, a practicing Buddhist, asks you to let the fish very slowly cook on one side, uncovered, in a shallow bath, which is why the French call this a l'unilateral. I guess I'm just not Zen enough, because every time I tried the technique, after 20 or 25 minutes of waiting, I was tempted to either turn up the heat, turn over the fish, or both. Because I'm not nearly as smart (or patient) as Ripert, it took far too long for me to realize that the method that better suits my temperament is a common one: Cover the fish. The most important ingredient, besides the fish, is the delicately seasoned Shaoxing cooking wine, which can be found in Asian supermarkets. It's worth trying to find, but you can substitute Japanese mirin, dry sherry, or other Chinese rice wine, although you may need to adjust the seasoning with vinegar before you eat it. Just don't use generic "cooking wine" you see in mainstream supermarkets; you'll regret that, believe me.

1 (6- to 8-ounce) halibut fillet (about 1 inch thick)
Kosher or sea salt
Freshly ground black pepper
½ cup Shaoxing Chinese cooking wine, plus more as needed
½ cup water
1-inch piece fresh ginger, peeled and finely grated (about 1 tablespoon)

1 green cardamom pod
2 small or 1 medium carrot, peeled, cut in half lengthwise, and then cut into ¼-inch half-moons (about ½ cup)
2 to 3 very small baby bok choy, quartered lengthwise
1 teaspoon unseasoned rice vinegar, or more to taste (optional)

Pat dry the fish with paper towels and season it on both sides with salt and pepper. Pour the wine and water into a small skillet over medium-high heat and bring to a boil. Whisk in the ginger, toss in the cardamom pod, and decrease the heat until the liquid is barely simmering. Place the halibut in the skillet and scatter the carrots around it, adding more wine, if necessary, until the liquid comes about ½ inch up the side of the fish. Cover and cook until the halibut is just barely cooked through and flakes easily with a fork, and the carrot pieces are just tender, 10 to 12 minutes.

Use a spatula to transfer the halibut to a plate, then use a slotted spoon to transfer the carrots. Cover the plate loosely with a piece of aluminum foil.

Increase the heat under the skillet to medium-high and add the baby bok choy, tossing and swirling them in the bubbling liquid until the green sections are wilted and the white sections have just started to soften but are still somewhat crisp, 4 to 5 minutes. Use the slotted spoon or tongs to transfer the baby bok choy to the plate, too.

Increase the heat to high and let the liquid continue boiling vigorously, swirling occasionally, until it becomes a sticky glaze, 3 to 4 minutes. Taste, and if the glaze is too sweet, add the vinegar to taste. Immediately pour the glaze over the fish and eat.

CHAPTER 5
TACOS

· ·

Many Americans' vision of tacos involves ground beef, shredded Cheddar, crispy shells, and something by Old El Paso. And that was certainly true for me as a kid in West Texas. My taco tastes have matured, thanks to multiple visits to Mexico and a proliferation of taco trucks in cities such as Austin, Los Angeles, and Portland, Oregon.

As a result, for many years now, I've been such a taco freak that anytime I taste something good, I think: How would that be wrapped up in freshly made corn tortillas (which I strongly prefer over flour tortillas), with salsa and maybe some pickled onions thrown in?

Tacos are one of my standby dishes when I want to use up leftovers, but more and more I've come to love making them (more or less) from scratch, paying attention to the way particular meats, seafood, or vegetables pair with specific salsas and other ingredients. I always try to have something rich, something sharp, something spicy, and something crunchy.

Besides those flavors, my favorite thing about tacos can summed up in two words: no utensils.

HOMEMADE CORN TORTILLAS

Makes about 24 (4- to 5-inch) tortillas

I used to have such trouble making corn tortillas at home, using instant masa flour, that I always assumed the good ones I encountered in Texas and Mexico must have been made from scratch, and I pictured the cooks soaking the dried corn in lime, grinding it by hand, that sort of thing. Then on a trip to Mexico City a few years ago, practically every restaurant kitchen my sister and I saw, even those where the tortillas were beautifully flaky and delicious, had the same bags of Maseca brand masa that I used. Why I couldn't get the results they did, using the same thing (which is really nothing more than corn treated with lime)? I called my friend, Mexican Cultural Institute cooking teacher Patricia Jinich, for a lesson, which turned into two, which turned into further emails and phone calls. It seems I wasn't using enough water. Granted, I was following the proportions on the package, but Pati showed me that when I increased the proportion of water, the tortillas pressed more easily and looked smoother on the edges. Most important, when following her other techniques, such as her double-flip method, the tortillas puffed up when I cooked them: a sign that they had the internal layers required of a good corn tortilla. Making corn tortillas at home takes a little practice (and, of course a cast-iron tortilla press, which costs less than $20). If you don't have access to good Latin markets, it's worth it.

2 cups masa harina, Maseca brand preferred
1 teaspoon fine sea salt

1¾ to 2¼ cups water

Cut 2 circles the size of the tortilla press's plates out of a heavy-duty resealable plastic bag, open the press, and set one on the bottom plate.

Preheat an ungreased griddle, large skillet (preferably nonstick), or Mexican comal over medium-high heat for at least 10 minutes.

In a large mixing bowl, stir together the masa and salt. Pour in 1¾ cups water and thoroughly combine, using a wooden spoon at first and then kneading the dough with your hands for a few minutes. It should feel tacky and moist, like fresh Play-Doh, but not wet and sticky. If it feels too dry, add another ¼ cup of water.

Pull off a golf ball–size piece of dough and roll it into a ball 1 to 1½ inches in diameter. Cover the remaining dough with a damp paper towel or cloth as you work. Place the ball in the middle of the plastic circle lining the bottom plate of the tortilla press, put the other

plastic circle on top, and close the press, clamping down and gently pressing until the tortilla is 4 to 5 inches in diameter and ⅛ to 1/16 inch thick.

Examine the tortilla: If the edges are very jagged, the dough is too dry. Return the dough to the bowl, knead it back into the rest of the mass, and add a tablespoon or two of water, and try the test again.

When the dough is moist enough to form a clean-edged tortilla, peel off the tortilla in its plastic wrap from the press, lay it on one hand, and carefully peel off the plastic wrap from the top. Switch it to the other hand, and peel off the plastic from the other side. Gently lay it on the griddle or comal in one decisive move. The aim is to get it flat on the surface without it folding or breaking, but this can take some practice. Resist the temptation to move the tortilla once it has hit the hot surface, even if it has folded, and just try to do better the next time.

Let the tortilla cook on the first side for only 15 to 25 seconds, or just until you can easily slide a spatula underneath. Flip the tortilla over; the side now on top should be mottled with spots of pale white and maybe a speck or two of brown. On the second side, let it cook for about 1 minute, until it is speckled brown on the bottom, then flip again.

Your tortilla should now start to puff up in spots. If it doesn't, poke at it with your finger all around; this can sometimes cause it to puff. Once it puffs, cook it for another 20 to 30 seconds, or until speckled brown on the bottom. Transfer it to a cloth-lined tortilla warmer, or to a clean towel folded and wrapped inside foil.

Repeat until all the tortillas are made. Resist the urge to form all the dough into balls before flattening them, because the dough will dry out more quickly. (Once you get the hang of it, though, you can start forming one tortilla while another one cooks.) Use what you want immediately (no need to warm the freshly made ones over a burner the way you do store-bought tortillas) and refrigerate the rest in a sealed plastic bag in the refrigerator for up to a week, or in the freezer for several months.

WORKING WITH CORN TORTILLAS

If you're able to get great, homemade corn tortillas in your neighborhood, consider yourself very lucky. Many of us have to be satisfied with whatever we can find at the supermarket. If there's not a decent Latin-foods section, we are stuck with something too tough and leathery (such as those sold by a nationwide natural-foods superstore chain) or thin and flimsy. No matter what the source, you need to heat the tortillas before using, to make sure they're nice and pliable.

For those of us with a gas stove, it's easy: Just turn on as many burners as you have tortillas to medium-high heat. Heat a tortilla on each burner for a minute or so on each side, until the tortillas start to puff and a few black spots form, using tongs to turn them. If you have an electric stove, heat the tortillas, one at a time, in a dry skillet over medium-low heat until they are pliable. Wrap the warm tortillas in a single packet of aluminum foil as you work.

Say you've done all that, and your tortillas are still too flimsy to hold your taco fillings. In that case, feel free to do what the pros do, and double them up.

AUSTIN-STYLE BREAKFAST TACOS

I have to admit, it was a little strange writing a recipe for breakfast tacos, as much as I love them, because I think of them as so free-form. In my college days in Austin, when I powered my way to class by eating a couple of these every morning, I would change up the order pretty much each time. Cheese and salsa are must-haves, but otherwise my favorite combination is potato, egg, and chorizo. But you can also add (or substitute) black beans, avocado, bacon, and the like, in whatever lineup gets you going. Leftover breakfast foods, such as hash browns, are welcome additions, too. This makes two hefty tacos: a hearty breakfast or brunch.

1 very small (3- to 4-ounce) potato of any variety, scrubbed but not peeled
2 eggs
1 link fresh Mexican chorizo (about 3 ounces)
2 (8-inch) flour tortillas

1 teaspoon extra-virgin olive oil
1 ounce Monterey Jack cheese, grated
¼ cup Blackened Salsa (page 16), Salsa Verde (page 14), or salsa of your choice

Line a large plate on one side with a folded paper towel.

Pierce the potato all over with a fork and microwave on High for 3 minutes. Let cool, then cut into ½-inch pieces.

Break the eggs into a small bowl and whisk to combine.

Put a small skillet over medium heat. Slice open the chorizo casing and squeeze out the sausage into the pan. Break it up with a spoon and sauté until it browns and becomes crisp, 3 to 4 minutes. Add the potato pieces, stir to combine, and cook for a minute or so until the potato is colored from the chorizo. Transfer to one side of the prepared plate and cover with a piece of aluminum foil to keep warm.

Warm the tortillas (see page 81) and wrap them in foil to keep warm.

Wipe out the skillet, return it to medium heat, and pour in the oil. When it shimmers, add the eggs, stirring and cooking them until they are set but still moist, 1 to 2 minutes. Immediately scoop them onto the other side of the plate with the chorizo-potato mixture and return the foil to cover. Lay the tortillas out on a plate. Divide the chorizo-potato mixture between the tortillas. Top with the eggs and a sprinkling of cheese. Close the tortillas to let the cheese melt slightly, then open them, spoon the salsa evenly over the other ingredients, close, and eat.

TACOS DE HUEVOS

· ·

These simple, satisfying tacos were inspired by breakfast tacos in Austin, roasted sweet potatoes sold by street vendors in Mexico City, and the need for a quick, spicy meal to be devoured in front of the TV after a long workday.

· ·

1 small (5- to 6-ounce) sweet potato
1 tablespoon extra-virgin olive oil
2 eggs
Kosher or sea salt
Freshly ground black pepper

2 corn tortillas, preferably homemade (page 84)
¼ cup Blackened Salsa (page 16) or salsa of your choice
¼ cup Citrus-Pickled Onions (page 19)
2 tablespoons chopped fresh cilantro leaves

Preheat the oven to 425°F.

Use a fork or sharp knife to prick the sweet potato in several places. Place on a piece of aluminum foil and bake until the sweet potato is tender and can be easily squeezed, 40 to 60 minutes. (Alternatively, to speed up the process, the pricked sweet potato can be microwaved on High for 1 minute, then carefully transferred to the oven on a piece of foil. Bake until the potato is tender, 25 to 35 minutes.)

Meanwhile, pour the oil into a medium skillet over medium-low heat. Break the eggs into two small bowls. Carefully tip each egg from the bowl into the skillet. Season with salt and pepper, decrease the heat to low, cover, and cook until the tops of the eggs have barely filmed over with white and the yolks are still runny, about 2 minutes. Warm the tortillas (see page 81) and wrap in foil to keep warm.

Discard the sweet potato's foil wrap; peel the potato, if desired, and cut it into ½-inch slices or chunks. Season with salt and pepper.

Lay the tortillas out on a plate. Use a spatula to move each egg to one of the tortillas and divide the sweet potato between the two tacos. Top each portion with half of the salsa, pickled onions, and cilantro, and eat.

TACOS WITH MUSHROOMS AND CHILE-CARAMELIZED ONIONS

Carnivores need a veggie break now and then, and this taco satisfies. The moist mushrooms stand in for the meat, the onions pack a sweet-spicy punch, goat cheese adds a touch of tart richness, good old lettuce gives the crunch, and a final drizzle of Salsa Verde (page 14) reminds you that, well, every taco can benefit from a final drizzle of salsa.

1 tablespoon extra-virgin olive oil
½ teaspoon ground ancho, chipotle, or other chile
¼ teaspoon ground cumin
¼ teaspoon ground cinnamon
1 small red onion, thinly sliced (about 1½ cups)
3 cloves garlic, thinly sliced
½ teaspoon kosher or coarse sea salt
½ teaspoon sugar

3 or 4 corn tortillas, preferably homemade (page 84)
6 ounces oyster, cremini, hen of the woods, or other meaty mushrooms, cut into large pieces
1 ounce soft goat cheese, cut into small pieces
2 large leaves romaine lettuce, shredded
1 to 2 tablespoons Salsa Verde (page 14) or salsa of your choice

Heat the oil in a large skillet over medium heat. When it shimmers, sprinkle in the ground ancho, cumin, and cinnamon and cook until the spices sizzle and are very fragrant, about 30 seconds. Toss in the onion slices, stirring to break them apart. Cook until the onion starts to soften, 3 to 4 minutes. Stir in the garlic, salt, and sugar. Decrease the heat to low and continue to cook, stirring occasionally, until the onions are very soft, about 10 minutes.

While the onions are cooking, warm the tortillas (see page 81) and wrap them in aluminum foil to keep warm.

Increase the heat under the skillet to medium-high, add the mushrooms, toss to combine, and cook, stirring occasionally, until the mushrooms exude their juices and are just tender, 4 to 5 minutes. Remove from the heat.

Lay the tortillas out on a plate. Divide the mushroom-onion mixture among the tortillas. Top each with a few pieces of goat cheese, a tablespoon or two of shredded lettuce, and a drizzle of salsa, and eat.

CHICKPEA, SPINACH, FETA, AND **PEPITA TACOS**

. . . .

I have to admit that making a vegetarian dinner is liberating. When I don't include meat, I feel entitled to splurge on other riches, in this case avocado and pumpkin seeds. Nonetheless, these veggie-packed tacos are proof that something can be hearty and healthful at the same time.

. . . .

3 or 4 corn tortillas, preferably homemade (page 84)
1 teaspoon extra-virgin olive oil
¼ teaspoon ground ancho chile
2 cloves garlic, thinly sliced
1 small shallot lobe, thinly sliced
1 small tomato, chopped (or substitute ⅓ cup canned crushed tomatoes in their juices)
⅓ cup cooked chickpeas, preferably homemade (page 47), drained and rinsed

¾ cup lightly packed spinach leaves, stacked, rolled, and thinly sliced
Kosher or sea salt
Freshly ground black pepper
½ avocado, peeled, seeded, and cut into chunks
1 ounce feta cheese, crumbled
1 tablespoon roasted pumpkin seeds (pepitas)
Hot pepper sauce, such as Tabasco
½ lime

Warm the tortillas (see page 81) and wrap them in aluminum foil to keep warm.

Pour the oil into a medium skillet over medium heat. When the oil starts to shimmer, add the ground ancho, stir to combine, and cook until it sizzles and becomes very fragrant, about 30 seconds. Add the garlic and shallot and cook until the vegetables start to soften and slightly brown, 4 to 6 minutes.

Stir in the tomato and chickpeas and cook, stirring occasionally, until the tomato softens and starts to break down. Add the spinach and cook until the spinach wilts, 1 to 2 minutes. Season with salt and pepper to taste.

Lay the tortillas out on a plate and divide the chickpea-spinach mixture among them. Top with the avocado and feta and sprinkle with the pumpkin seeds. Dash a little Tabasco on each taco, squeeze the lime over them, and eat.

Note: To roast the pumpkin seeds, spread them in a single layer on a baking sheet. Bake at 375°F for 5 to 7 minutes, until the seeds are very fragrant. Immediately transfer to a plate to stop the cooking and allow the seeds to cool completely.

PASTORAL TACOS

If you haven't eaten tacos in Mexico City, then as far as I'm concerned, you haven't really eaten tacos. Countless joints there specialize in tacos al pastor, carved off a spit like the shawarma from which it is derived, but with the delectable addition of pineapple (and with tortillas, naturally, instead of pita). They usually make a bit of a show of it, too: At El Califa, my sister and I watched the taco guy hold a plate with two tortillas on it in one hand, then use a long knife in the other to swipe off a chunk of pork, which fell right onto one of the tortillas. He quickly reached higher and sliced off a bit of the pineapple ring that was sitting on top of the spit, catching the fruit, too, on the tortilla. One of El Califa's other specialties is a steak cutlet taco: The single piece of meat is longer than the tortilla, but it's so tender it folds up inside and you can bite through it with your teeth. I like to combine the two ideas into one: using a thin cutlet of pork that I quickly marinate in pineapple juice and combining the traditional garnishes of onion, cilantro, pineapple, and lime into a quick salsa.

3 (2-ounce) pork cutlets, trimmed of excess fat (or substitute a 6-ounce boneless center-cut pork chop)
1 tablespoon distilled white vinegar
2 tablespoons fresh pineapple juice
½ teaspoon pimenton (smoked Spanish paprika)
½ teaspoon crumbled dried pasilla or ancho chile (or substitute red pepper flakes)
½ teaspoon kosher or coarse sea salt, plus more to taste
½ teaspoon freshly ground black pepper
½ cup fresh pineapple chunks, cut into ½-inch cubes
1 tablespoon chopped fresh cilantro leaves
1 large shallot lobe, finely chopped
½ medium jalapeño chile, stemmed, seeded, and chopped
½ lime
3 corn tortillas, preferably homemade (page 84)
1 teaspoon extra-virgin olive oil

Place each pork cutlet between two pieces of plastic wrap and pound to a thickness of about ⅛ inch. (If you are using a boneless center-cut pork chop, first steady it flat on the cutting board with one hand and then, with the knife parallel to the cutting board, slice it into thirds horizontally. Then place each third between two pieces of plastic wrap and pound to ⅛ inch thick.)

Combine the vinegar, pineapple juice, pimenton, chile, salt, and pepper in a large resealable plastic food storage bag; mix well, then add the cutlets. Press the air out of the bag and seal; massage the marinade into the meat. Let sit for at least 10 minutes or up to an hour, while you make the salsa and warm the tortillas.

Combine the pineapple, cilantro, shallot, and jalapeño in a small bowl. Squeeze the lime juice into the bowl. Add salt to taste and mix well.

Warm the tortillas (see page 81) and wrap them in aluminum foil to keep warm.

Pour the oil into a large skillet set over medium-high heat. When it starts to shimmer, remove the cutlets from the marinade, shake off any excess, and place in the skillet. Sprinkle lightly with a little more salt, then cook until lightly browned on one side, 1 to 2 minutes. Turn them over, sprinkle lightly with salt, and cook until browned on the other side and just cooked throughout, another 1 to 2 minutes. Turn off the heat and let the cutlets rest for a minute.

Lay the tortillas out on a plate. Place one cutlet on each tortilla. Top each with pineapple salsa, and eat.

Note: If your pork is too firm or chewy to easily fold up whole in the tortilla, feel free to cut it into strips or chunks.

KOREAN SHORT RIB TACOS

This recipe is as much of a mash-up as the idea of Korean tacos in the first place, made famous and trendy by the Kogi BBQ truck in Los Angeles. I took the idea of using prune juice to tenderize and marinate short ribs from Rozanne Gold's *Recipes 1-2-3* and the idea to include Asian pear, scallions, and sesame seeds from Joanne Chang of Boston's Myers + Chang restaurant. This makes enough short ribs for three or four meals, depending on your appetite. (In addition to these tacos, you can toss the short ribs with egg noodles, eat over polenta, or layer into a particularly sophisticated take on nachos.)

SHORT RIBS
3 pounds bone-in beef short ribs
Kosher or sea salt
2 tablespoons olive oil
1 Asian pear
½ cup prune juice
½ cup water
¼ cup soy sauce
¼ cup mirin (Japanese cooking wine)
2 tablespoons sake
2 (1-inch) pieces fresh ginger, peeled and smashed
4 whole star anise
¼ teaspoon black peppercorns

TACOS
3 or 4 corn tortillas, preferably homemade (page 84)
⅓ cup Cabbage and Pear Kimchi (page 18) or your favorite store-bought version
1 scallion, white and green parts, diagonally sliced ¼ inch thick
1 teaspoon sesame seeds
Asian-style hot sauce, such as Sriracha sauce (optional)

To make the short ribs, season the ribs generously with salt. Pour the oil into a 4- to 6-quart pot over medium-high heat. When it starts to shimmer, add the short ribs in a single layer, being careful not to crowd and working in batches if necessary. Sear until deeply browned on all sides, about 4 minutes per side. Transfer the ribs to a platter. Pour off and discard the extra fat in the pot from the ribs, leaving the browned bits in the bottom of the pot for flavor.

Core and remove the stem from the Asian pear and cut it into quarters. Thinly slice one quarter and reserve it for the tacos. Run the remaining three-quarters across the large holes of a box grater. Add the pear to a medium bowl, and stir in the prune juice, water, soy sauce, mirin, sake, ginger, star anise, and black peppercorns.

Return the ribs to the pot, set over medium-high heat, and pour the prune juice mixture over the ribs. Bring the mixture to a boil and decrease the heat to low or medium-low, so that the liquid is at a bare simmer. Cover and cook until the meat is so tender it offers no resistance at all to a skewer inserted into the thickest part, 2 to 2½ hours. The short rib should stay in place and not be lifted up when you raise the skewer, and the meat should slip away from the bone.

Transfer the cooked short ribs to a bowl and cover with a piece of aluminum foil to keep them warm.

Pour the sauce through a fine-mesh strainer into a large measuring cup with a pouring spout and discard the solids. (If you'd like to defat the sauce, you can refrigerate it for an hour or two, until the fat congeals on the top; scrape it off and discard it.) Pour the sauce back into the pot over medium-high heat and cook the sauce, uncovered, at a vigorous bubble until it is very syrupy and reduced to about 1 cup, 20 to 30 minutes. Decrease the heat to low and cover the pot to keep the sauce warm.

To make the tacos, warm the tortillas (see page 85) and wrap them in aluminum foil to keep warm.

Remove any large strips of fat or gristle from the short ribs, then lightly shred the meat using forks or your fingers. Pour the sauce over the meat and toss to thoroughly coat it. Depending on the meatiness of your short ribs, you should have 2 to 3 cups of meat. Use ½ to ¾ cup for one serving of tacos, and reserve the rest of the meat for another two or three meals.

Transfer the warm tortillas to a dinner plate. Divide the short rib meat among them and top with kimchi, Asian pear, scallion, a sprinkle of sesame seeds, and a drizzle of hot sauce, and eat.

Refrigerate the leftover short ribs for up to a week in an airtight container, or freeze for several months.

COCHINITA PIBIL TACOS
WITH HABANERO SALSA

You've done the work to make the Yucatan-Style Slow-Roasted Pork (page 66) already, so now you get to take advantage of its depth of flavor and combine it with a fiery (and I mean that) salsa and Citrus-Pickled Onions (page 19) in these vibrant tacos. This recipe makes about ¼ cup of the salsa, and a little goes a long way, so you may have some left over. It will last for 2 weeks refrigerated in an airtight container, and you can use it on all manner of eggs and meats, and as a salad dressing base, but my favorite use might be to mash a tablespoon or two into the yolks of a half dozen hard-cooked eggs, along with mayo, for a party snack that puts the devil back into deviled eggs, for sure. (And yes, pickled onions are good on those babies, too.)

1 cup Yucatan-Style Slow-Roasted Pork (page 65), defrosted if frozen
1 habanero chile
1 clove garlic, unpeeled
4 corn tortillas, preferably homemade (page 84)
¼ cup lightly packed fresh cilantro leaves, coarsely chopped

1 scallion, white and green parts, coarsely chopped
Juice of 1 lime, plus more as needed
1 teaspoon extra-virgin olive oil
Kosher or sea salt
¼ cup Citrus-Pickled Onions (page 19)

Heat the pork in a small saucepan over medium heat, stirring occasionally, until hot, 4 to 5 minutes.

Char the habanero by holding it with tongs over the flame of a gas burner for several minutes, turning it as needed, until it is spotted black and blistered all over. Remove the loose outer layers of papery skin from the garlic clove but leave the tight inner peel intact. Char it over the gas burner using the same technique, until it is completely blackened. (If you don't have a gas stove, broil the habanero and garlic clove a few inches from the broiler element, turning as needed to char them all over.)

Warm the tortillas (see page 81), then wrap in aluminum foil to keep warm.

Carefully stem the habanero, scrape out the seeds, and coarsely chop the flesh, preferably wearing plastic gloves to protect your fingers from the heat of the chile. Peel the garlic clove, coarsely chop it, and add it, along with about half the habanero, to the bowl of a food processor (preferably a mini one). Add the cilantro, scallion, lime juice, oil, and salt to taste and process until a loose sauce forms. Taste and add the rest of the habanero if you want the salsa to be spicier, and add more lime juice and/or salt if needed.

Lay the tortillas out on a plate. Divide the pork equally among the tortillas, top with the pickled onions and just a little bit of the salsa (be judicious until you know how much you can handle), and eat.

SMOKED TURKEY TACOS
WITH MOLE VERDE

After moving from Austin to Boston, I would periodically get such a jones for Tex-Mex food that nothing would satisfy it but a casserole dish full of enchiladas stuffed with chunks of smoked turkey and slathered in a spicy-sweet green mole sauce. They had been a favorite of mine at Z'Tejas, at the time a funky place on 6th Street, but now a small chain with outposts in Texas, Utah, California, Arizona, and Washington State. I was thrilled when the *Austin American-Statesman* ran a recipe for the enchiladas a few years after I left town. It enabled me to invite over a mix of fellow Tex-pats and native New Englanders and have everyone marveling at the revelation that is a chocolate-free mole sauce. All these years later, the revelation for me was how easily they morphed into soft tacos, still with that unusual combination of smoked turkey breast and mole verde. For this, the smoked turkey should be cut from a very thick slice, so either buy a whole or half smoked breast yourself and cut it from there, or ask your deli to custom-cut a ½-inch slice or two.

MOLE VERDE SAUCE
4 tomatillos, husks removed and rinsed (about 6 ounces)

1 jalapeño chile

⅔ cup coarsely chopped fresh cilantro, lightly packed, plus 3 sprigs for garnish

½ teaspoon kosher or coarse salt, plus more as needed

¼ teaspoon chili powder

¼ teaspoon ground cumin

2 tablespoons honey

2 teaspoons extra-virgin olive oil 5 tablespoons shelled raw pumpkin seeds (pepitas)

TACOS
3 corn tortillas, preferably homemade (page 84)

1 teaspoon extra-virgin olive oil

2 large or 3 small shallot lobes, thinly sliced

4 ounces boneless smoked turkey breast, cut into ½-inch chunks

2 tablespoons water

1 to 2 ounces Monterey Jack cheese, shredded

To make the mole verde, bring a 2-quart saucepan of water to a rolling boil over high heat. Carefully drop the tomatillos into the water and boil them for 5 minutes, then use a slotted spoon to transfer them to a blender along with 2 tablespoons of the boiling water (discard the rest). Stem, seed, and coarsely chop the jalapeño; reserve the seeds. Add the jalapeño to the blender, along with the cilantro, salt, chili powder, cumin, honey, oil, and 4 tablespoons of the pumpkin seeds. Remove the center cap from the top of the blender lid to allow the heat to escape and place a dish towel over it to prevent any splatters; pulse to puree until smooth. Taste, and add more

salt if needed. If you want it spicier, add some of the reserved jalapeño seeds and puree again, repeating until you've reached the desired heat level.

To make the tacos, warm the tortillas (see page 85) and wrap them in aluminum foil to keep warm.

Heat the oil in a small skillet over medium heat. When the oil shimmers, add the shallots and cook, stirring occasionally, until softened and starting to brown, 4 to 6 minutes. Add the smoked turkey and water, cover, and cook for another 2 minutes, or until heated through.

To assemble, lay the tortillas out on a plate. Divide the turkey-shallot mixture among the tortillas, spoon a tablespoon or two of the mole verde sauce on top and sprinkle with the cheese, the remaining tablespoon of pumpkin seeds, and the cilantro sprigs, and eat.

Note: To roast the pumpkin seeds, spread them in a single layer on a baking sheet. Bake at 375°F for 5 to 7 minutes, until the seeds are very fragrant.

Immediately transfer to a plate to stop the cooking and allow the seeds to cool completely.

Note: This makes twice as much sauce as you will need, but it will keep in an airtight container for up to 2 weeks. Use on another batch of tacos, or on scrambled eggs on toast, grilled steak, chicken and rice, and more.

DUCK BREAST TACOS
WITH PLUM SALSA

You know you've got a taco problem when you make a duck breast recipe from a destined-to-be-classic Chinese cookbook and think, "Wouldn't these be good in tortillas?" Yes, that's what happened to me when I tried Eileen Yin-Fei Lo's simple baked duck breasts from *Mastering the Art of Chinese Cooking*. I served them for a Chinese dinner that night, but pretty soon I was playing around with a riff on five-spice powder, combining Asian and Mexican ingredients and rubbing them into the breasts before using Lo's baking technique. A sweet, sour, and spicy plum salsa was just the thing to cut through and complement the deep flavors of the rich duck.

1 whole star anise

1 teaspoon dried oregano (preferably Mexican)

½ teaspoon Szechuan peppercorns

½ teaspoon ground ancho or other chile

½ teaspoon kosher or coarse sea salt, plus more to taste

¼ teaspoon ground cinnamon

2 boneless, skin-on duck breast halves (6 to 8 ounces each)

3 or 4 corn tortillas, preferably homemade (page 84)

½ jalapeño chile, stemmed and seeded (seeds reserved)

1 barely ripe black or red plum, pitted and cut into ½-inch pieces

1 small shallot lobe, thinly sliced

1 tablespoon lightly packed fresh cilantro leaves, chopped

3 large fresh mint leaves, chopped

2 teaspoons freshly squeezed lime juice

1 teaspoon extra-virgin olive oil

Using a spice grinder (such as a coffee grinder reserved for spices), grind the star anise, dried oregano, and Szechuan peppercorns to a fine powder. Dump into a small bowl and stir in the ground ancho, salt, and cinnamon.

Pat dry the duck breasts with a paper towel. Use a sharp knife to cut through just the skin and fat, without piercing the meat, in 1-inch intervals, then repeat the cuts at a 90° angle to make a crosshatch pattern all across the skin. Sprinkle the spice mixture all over the duck breasts. Pack in heavy-duty resealable plastic bags, squeezing as much air out as possible, and refrigerate for several hours or as long as 24 hours.

Preheat the oven to 450°F.

In a small roasting pan lined with aluminum foil, roast the duck breasts skin side up for 10 minutes. Increase the heat to 550°F and turn the breasts skin side down. Roast until much of the fat has rendered and the skin is browned and crisp, 8 to 10 minutes. Transfer to a plate, pour off the extra duck fat from the pan and reserve for another use. Let the duck breasts rest for at least 10 minutes. (If desired, wrap one of the duck breasts in plastic wrap and refrigerate it for up to 1 week for a later meal.)

Warm the tortillas (see page 85) and wrap them in aluminum foil to keep warm.

continued

DUCK BREAST TACOS with PLUM SALSA, continued

Meanwhile, make the salsa. Finely chop the jalapeño. In a small mixing bowl, combine the jalapeño with the plum, shallot, cilantro, mint, lime juice, oil, and a generous sprinkling of salt. Taste, add more salt if necessary; if you want more heat, add some of the reserved jalapeño seeds.

Lay the tortillas out on a plate. Cut the duck breast crosswise into ½-inch slices, place a couple of slices on each tortilla, top each with the plum salsa, and eat.

Note: I call for two duck breasts here, because it's difficult to make much less of this spice rub, but you can save one of the breasts for another day and another use (such as sliced cold on a salad).

CATFISH TACOS WITH CHIPOTLE SLAW

I'm as intimidated about making fish tacos for California friends as they would be to make chili for me. But I've learned the rules: No baking the fish, no guacamole (makes the fish soggy), no flour tortillas (although there's some dispute on that point)? And you should hear the unprintable things they say about versions that include mayonnaise! It just so happens that I agree on all those points, except for one, which my Cali-friends will discover when they read this: I have actually made pretty darn crisp catfish in the oven. When it's just you alone in the kitchen, and you don't feel like frying, I won't judge.

1 cup shredded red cabbage (about ¼ small head)
1 teaspoon kosher or coarse sea salt, plus more to taste
2 tablespoons Mexican crema or sour cream
1 teaspoon adobo sauce (from canned chipotle in adobo) or ½ teaspoon ground chipotle chile
6 ounces catfish fillet, cut crosswise into 2-inch strips

Freshly ground black pepper
1 egg
½ cup Japanese-style panko
Canola oil, for frying
3 corn tortillas, preferably homemade (page 84)
¼ cup Salsa Verde (page 14) or other tangy salsa
1 lime, cut into quarters
A few sprigs cilantro (optional)

Toss the cabbage and salt in a colander set over a plate or baking sheet, put a plate directly on the cabbage, and weight it down with a heavy object, such as a large can of tomatoes or beans, for at least 30 minutes. Drain the cabbage.

Lay out a couple of sheets of paper towels on your countertop. Transfer the cabbage to the paper towels. Roll up the paper towels and, holding it above a bowl, use your hands to squeeze the extra moisture out of the cabbage. Transfer the cabbage to a small bowl and add the crema and adobo sauce.

Season the catfish well on both sides with salt and pepper. Whisk the egg in a medium bowl until just combined; spread the panko on a plate. Dredge each piece of catfish first in the egg, then in the panko, packing the panko lightly onto the fish with your hands to get it to stick.

Line a plate with paper towels. Pour enough canola oil into a large cast-iron skillet to come to a depth of ½ inch and turn the heat to medium high. When

the oil starts to shimmer, add the fish and fry without turning until the panko crumbs are a deep golden brown, 2 to 4 minutes. Turn and fry until golden brown on the other side, another 2 to 4 minutes. Transfer the fish to the paper towel–lined plate. (Alternatively, preheat the oven to 425°F. After coating the fish, transfer it to a small rack set on a baking sheet and bake for 10 to 12 minutes, or until lightly golden brown and crisp.)

While the fish is frying or baking, warm the tortillas (see page 85) and wrap in aluminum foil to keep warm.

To make the tacos, lay the tortillas out on a plate. Divide the fish strips among the tortillas. Top with the chipotle slaw, salsa verde, a squeeze of lime, and cilantro, and eat.

SHRIMP TACOS WITH GRAPEFRUIT–BLACK BEAN SALSA

Shrimp and citrus make such a natural match, I often combine them in tacos, but they call out for something with a little heft, such as black beans. Depending on the size grapefruit you use, you'll probably have more than you need for this recipe, but that's not a problem. Just eat the remaining sections for breakfast with a little yogurt, for dessert instead of the oranges in the Yogurt Parfait with Mulled Red Wine Syrup (page 161), or in a smoothie with banana and milk. I like to sometimes double up the salsa on this taco, drizzling on a little Salsa Verde (page 14) in addition to the on-the-fly grapefruit–black bean salsa, but these tacos are plenty flavorful without it.

1 small or ½ large red grapefruit
¼ cup cooked black beans, preferably homemade (page 47), rinsed and drained
1 scallion, white and green parts, thinly sliced
1 small jalapeño, stemmed, seeded, and finely chopped
2 tablespoons fresh cilantro leaves, chopped
Kosher or sea salt
3 or 4 corn tortillas, preferably homemade (page 85)

2 teaspoons extra-virgin olive oil
½ teaspoon ground ancho chile
1 small shallot lobe, thinly sliced
1 plump clove garlic, thinly sliced
5 to 6 ounces large shrimp, peeled and deveined
2 tablespoons water
¼ cup Salsa Verde (page 14) (optional)
1 ounce feta cheese, crumbled

To section the grapefruit, slice off both ends of the grapefruit with a chef's knife. Stand the grapefruit on one end, hold it steady with one hand, and use the other to slice from the top edge downward along the curve of the fruit, cutting away both the peel and the pith but leaving as much of the flesh as possible. Working over a bowl to catch the juices, hold the grapefruit in one hand and use a paring knife in the other to cut between the sections, detaching each section of fruit from its surrounding membrane. Let the sections fall into the bowl as you work.

Reserve ½ cup of sections. Pour off the excess juice and save for another use, along with the extra grapefruit sections, if you have any. Add the beans, scallion, jalapeño, and cilantro to the grapefruit in the bowl, and season with salt to taste.

Warm the tortillas (see page 81) and wrap them in aluminum foil to keep warm.

Pour the oil into a medium skillet set over medium heat. When the oil shimmers, sprinkle in the ground ancho and cook for about 30 seconds, until the powder sizzles and becomes very fragrant. Add the shallot and garlic and sauté until the vegetables start to brown, 3 to 4 minutes.

Season the shrimp with salt. Add the shrimp and water to the skillet and stir-fry for 2 or 3 minutes, until the shrimp is opaque and firm.

Lay the tortillas out on a plate and divide the shrimp mixture among them. Top with the grapefruit–black bean salsa, salsa verde, and feta, and eat.

CHAPTER 6
PIZZA

. . . .

Why make pizza at home? It's a fair question, especially because most home cooks don't have access to a wood-fired brick oven like the one my brother-in-law built for my sister in Maine. The best pizzas cook at upwards of 800°F to 900°F, compared to residential ranges that top out at 500°F or maybe 550°F.

Still, I've long wanted to crack the code of home pizza-making, for one simple reason: I need to stave off gluttony. At my favorite pizza places, the size of the pie I order is the size I try to eat, dinner companions be damned. Ordering delivery pizza is even worse, unless I'm having a party, because there's no one to fight me for the slices, and there it all goes. So I need to make (and eat) smaller pizzas.

The answer, for me, lies in a broiler method promoted by Fat Duck chef Heston Blumenthal in his book *In Search of Perfection* and also mentioned by pizza guru Peter Reinhart in *American Pie*. Once I mastered it, and put my own twist on it, I could turn my attention to the second-most-important question: the toppings. As the best pizzaiolos will tell you, the key is to use high-quality ingredients, and not too much of them. Don't overload the crust.

Pizza has now entered my weeknight meal rotation. Every month or so I make a batch of dough and divide it into single-serving-size portions. After making one pie, I immediately freeze the rest of the dough balls, to be defrosted at will. Between the dough in my freezer and some of the pizza toppings (kimchi, red pepper chutney, lemon confit, and the like) in my refrigerator, it's now officially faster to make pizza at home than to wait for the delivery boy. It should go without saying that it's officially better, too.

NO-KNEAD PIZZA DOUGH

Makes 5 (8-inch) pizza crusts or 10 (5-inch) flatbreads

This simple technique, adapted from Jim Lahey of Co. pizza restaurant and Sullivan Street Bakery in New York, is based on his famous no-knead bread. It makes for a very sticky, loose dough that seems as if it won't be easy to work with, but is very forgiving and performs well with the broiler method featured in the pizza recipes that follow. This dough requires some planning: You can start it in the morning and make pizza that evening, or start it the night before you want pizza for dinner.

4 cups bread flour, plus more as needed
¼ teaspoon instant dry yeast (also known as rapid-rise or bread machine yeast)

1½ teaspoons fine sea salt
1½ cups water
Olive oil

Combine the flour, yeast, and salt in a large bowl. Add the water and stir until blended. Cover the bowl with plastic wrap and let it rest for 8 to 12 hours at room temperature (about 70°F).

After 8 hours, the dough will have risen and be bubbly on the surface. The timing is very forgiving here; you can let it continue bubbling and very slowly expanding for several more hours if you like. Transfer the dough to the refrigerator for about an hour before dividing, so it's easier to work with.

Lightly rub your hands and work counter with olive oil. Turn out the dough onto the counter in one piece. Lightly dust it with flour and fold the dough on itself a few times, adding more flour if needed, until it comes together and holds its shape when you gather it into a ball. Cut into 5 equal pieces (for pizza), about 6 ounces apiece, or 10 equal pieces (for flatbread), about 3 ounces apiece.

Refrigerate or freeze what you're not going to use right away. Transfer the balls to individual freezer-safe plastic food storage bags, drizzle with olive oil, and turn the dough to coat it in the oil. Refrigerate for up to 3 days or freeze for up to 3 months.

Sprinkle the piece(s) you are going to use immediately with flour and transfer it to a lightly floured baking sheet. Cover with a towel or plastic wrap and let rise for about 1 hour.

Proceed with one of the pizza recipes on pages 106 to 118 or to the flatbread recipe on page 115.

Note: If you have refrigerated the dough, remove it from the refrigerator and let it rise for about 1 hour. If you have frozen the dough, defrost in the refrigerator for 8 to 12 hours, then transfer it to the counter to rise for an hour. The dough should be pliable and able to be easily stretched into shape.

NO-KNEAD PIZZA DOUGH WITH SPELT

Makes 5 (8-inch) pizza crusts or 10 (5-inch) flatbreads

When I told Sam Fromartz, a fantastic home baker who blogs at Chewswise.com, that I was playing around with pizza doughs, he persuaded me to try his take, which uses spelt, an ancient variety of wheat with a wonderfully nutty flavor and without the bitterness of whole wheat flour. Spelt is a little tricky to work with because it stretches very easily, but the addition of white bread flour brings structure. This no-knead dough, based on versions by Jim Lahey and Peter Reinhart, benefits from a long rise, preferably overnight. The result is a very flavorful dough, perfect for home pizza-making. Like the No-Knead Pizza Dough (page 104), it is sticky and loose, but comes together in a beautiful crust. It also requires a little forethought: You can make the dough in the evening for use the next day, or in the morning to use in the evening.

1½ cups whole spelt flour
2½ cups white bread flour, plus more as needed
2 teaspoons fine sea salt
½ teaspoon instant dry yeast (also known as rapid-rise or bread machine yeast)

1½ cups water
2 tablespoons extra-virgin olive oil, plus more as needed

Combine the flours, salt, and yeast in a large bowl.

Pour the water and oil into another bowl or measuring cup, pour the liquid into the flour mixture, and stir until blended.

Lightly coat a large clean bowl with olive oil and transfer the dough to the oiled bowl. Turn the dough to coat with oil. Cover with plastic wrap and let the dough rise for 8 to 12 hours at room temperature (about 70°F).

After 8 hours, the dough should have risen and be bubbly on the surface. The timing is very forgiving here; you can let it continue bubbling and very slowly expanding for several more hours if you like. Transfer the dough to the refrigerator for about an hour before dividing, so it's easier to work with. Lightly rub your hands and work counter with olive oil. Turn out the dough onto the counter in one piece. Lightly dust it with flour and fold it onto itself a few times, adding more flour if necessary, until the dough comes together and holds its shape when you form it into a ball. Cut into 5 equal pieces (for

pizza), about 6 ounces apiece, or 10 equal pieces (for flatbread), about 3 ounces apiece.

Refrigerate or freeze what you're not going to use right away. Transfer the balls to individual freezer-safe plastic food storage bags, drizzle with olive oil, and turn the dough to coat it in the oil. Refrigerate for up to 3 days or freeze for up to 3 months.

Sprinkle the piece(s) you are going to use immediately with flour and transfer to a lightly floured baking sheet. Cover with a towel or plastic wrap and let rise for about 1 hour.

Proceed with one of the pizza recipes on pages 106 to 118 or the flatbread recipe on page 115.

Note: If you have refrigerated the dough, remove it from the refrigerator and let it rise for about 1 hour. If you have frozen the dough, defrost in the refrigerator for 8 to 12 hours, then transfer it to the counter to rise for an hour. The dough should be pliable and able to be easily stretched into shape.

SMOKY PIZZA MARGHERITA

The only liberties I've taken with the classic margherita is to let one of my favorite pizza cheeses, smoked mozzarella, provide that extra, haunting flavor, to echo the smoke from a wood-burning pizza oven. And, of course, there are the 12-Hour Tomatoes (page 2) that I hope you have in your fridge just waiting for this moment to shine. (If you don't, substitute ⅓ cup canned diced tomatoes, preferably San Marzano, drained, plus a little salt and pepper to taste.)

1 (6-ounce) ball No-Knead Pizza Dough (page 104) or No-Knead Pizza Dough with Spelt (page 105)
All-purpose flour
3 large or 4 or 5 small 12-Hour Tomatoes (page 2), drained and chopped (about ⅓ cup)

2 ounces smoked mozzarella, cut into ¼-inch slices
5 large basil leaves, stacked, rolled, and thinly sliced
1 tablespoon extra-virgin olive oil

If the dough has been refrigerated, transfer it to the countertop to let it rise for about 1 hour before making pizza.

Preheat the broiler with the rack set 5 inches from the element or flame. If you are using a cast-iron skillet or griddle pan for the pizza, set it over medium-high heat until it gets smoking hot, about 15 minutes. Transfer the skillet (turned upside down) or griddle pan to the broiler. If you are using a baking stone, heat it in a 500°F oven for an hour, then carefully transfer it to the broiler.

To shape the dough, dust a work surface liberally with flour and put the ball of dough on it. Sprinkle with flour and knead a few times until the dough comes together and holds its shape when you form it into a ball. Add more flour if necessary. Form it into an 8-inch round by pressing from the center out toward the edges, leaving a 1-inch border thicker than the rest.

Make sure you have all the topping ingredients measured out and ready before you assemble the pizza, because once you place the dough on the cooking surface you can't easily move it.

Open the oven or broiler door, and quickly slide out the rack with the cooking surface (skillet, griddle pan, or baking stone) on it. Pick up the dough and quickly transfer it to the cooking surface, pressing it back into shape if need be, while being careful not to touch the cooking surface with your fingers.

Scatter the tomatoes on the dough, then the mozzarella pieces. Broil for 3 to 5 minutes, until the crust has puffed up around the edges and blackened in spots, the tomatoes are browned in spots and the mozzarella is melted.

Remove the pizza with a wooden or metal peel or a thin square of cardboard, transfer it to a cutting board, and let it rest for a few minutes. Sprinkle the pizza with the basil, drizzle the olive oil on top, cut the pizza into quarters, transfer it to a plate, and eat.

KIMCHI, HAM, AND FRIED EGG PIZZA

I make fried rice with kimchi, ham, and egg so often that you'd think this pizza combination would've occurred to me in a flash. It almost did, but not quite: I knew I wanted to make a kimchi and ham pizza, but it wasn't until I hosted a pizza party and friends tasted it that I asked, "What does it need?" One guest said, "An egg?" Of course! Why didn't I think of that? I tried it again, and that runny-yolk richness pulled everything together. It always does. Now I wouldn't have it any other way.

1 teaspoon extra-virgin olive oil
1 egg
Kosher or sea salt
Freshly ground black pepper
All-purpose flour
1 (6-ounce) ball No-Knead Pizza Dough (page 104)
    or No-Knead Pizza Dough with Spelt (page 105)

⅓ cup Cabbage and Pear Kimchi (page 18) or
    your favorite store-bought kimchi, squeezed to
    remove excess liquid
2 ounces cured, smoked ham, cut into ½-inch chunks
1 scallion, white and green parts, thinly sliced on
    the diagonal
1 teaspoon toasted sesame oil

If the dough has been refrigerated, transfer it to the countertop to let it rise for about 1 hour before making pizza.

Preheat the broiler with the rack set 5 inches from the element or flame. If you are using a cast-iron skillet or griddle pan for the pizza, set it over medium-high heat until it gets smoking hot, about 15 minutes. Transfer the skillet (turned upside down) or griddle pan to the broiler. If you are using a baking stone, heat it in a 500°F oven for an hour, then carefully transfer it to the broiler.

To fry the egg, pour the oil into a small skillet over medium-low heat. Break the egg into a small bowl, then carefully tip the egg from the bowl into the skillet. Season with salt and pepper, decrease the heat to low, cover, and cook until the top of the egg has barely filmed over with white and the yolk is still runny, about 2 minutes. Transfer the egg to a plate.

To shape the dough, dust a work surface liberally with flour and put the ball of dough on it. Sprinkle with flour and knead a few times until the dough comes together and holds its shape when you form it into a ball. Add more flour if necessary. Form it into an 8-inch round by pressing from the center out

toward the edges, leaving a 1-inch border thicker than the rest.

Make sure you have all the topping ingredients measured out and ready before you assemble the pizza, because once you place the dough on the cooking surface you can't easily move it.

Open the oven or broiler door, and quickly slide out the rack with the cooking surface (skillet, griddle pan, or baking stone) on it. Pick up the dough and quickly transfer it to the cooking surface, pressing it back into shape if need be, while being careful not to touch the cooking surface with your fingers.

Scatter the kimchi on top of the dough, leaving a 1-inch margin. Sprinkle on the ham and scallion.

Broil the pizza for 3 to 5 minutes, until the crust has puffed up around the edges and blackened in spots.

Remove the pizza with a wooden or metal peel or a square of cardboard, and transfer it to a cutting board. Let it rest for a few minutes, then transfer the fried egg to the center of the pizza, drizzle with the sesame oil, cut the pizza into quarters, transfer to a plate, and eat.

BROILING PIZZA

I cobbled together this technique from advances by Fat Duck chef Heston Blumenthal and *American Pie* author Peter Reinhart, and some consultation with Jim Lahey of Co. pizza in New York. The basic idea is this: With a blazing hot cast-iron skillet (turned upside down) or a long-preheated baking stone on the bottom and the flame of a broiler on the top, you can approximate the searing heat of a pizza oven, resulting in a pie that cooks in about 3 minutes. Because there are such varieties in home oven broilers—some, like mine, are in separate drawers below the oven, while others are at the top of the main oven chamber, and still others are on the side— I suggest that you experiment with various pans. My broiler is tight enough that a deep cast-iron skillet is too tall and gets the pizza too close to the flame, so I use a flat cast-iron griddle pan sometimes and a baking stone others.

The trickiest thing of all might be sliding the topped pizza onto the cooking surface without using a peel, which can require lots of cornmeal to keep the dough from sticking. The problem is that cornmeal (or flour or semolina) will start to smoke quickly (especially if you're making more than one pizza). You'd think parchment paper might be the key, but I find it tends to make for an underdone crust under the broiler. With Lahey's encouragement, I have taken to just picking up the dough and laying it directly on the hot skillet or stone, then ever-so-quickly adding the toppings and pushing the pizza under the broiler. The result is a fantastic crust that takes a little practice to master.

HERE'S WHAT YOU DO:

1. Prepare the broiler. Remove the broiler pan assembly if you have one, then set the oven to broil. Arrange the broiler rack so that your cooking surface—the back of a large cast-iron skillet, a flat cast-iron griddle pan, or a baking stone—is about 5 inches from the flame or broiler element. (You want the pizza itself to be about 4 inches from the broiler flame or element.)

2. Prepare the cooking surface. If you are using a cast-iron skillet or griddle pan, set it over medium-high heat until it gets smoking hot, about 15 minutes. Transfer the skillet (turned upside down) or griddle pan to the broiler while you prepare the pizza. If you are using a baking stone, heat it in a 500°F oven for an hour, then carefully transfer it to the broiler.

3. Shape the dough. Dust a work surface liberally with flour and put the ball of dough on it. Sprinkle with flour and knead a few times until the dough is no longer too sticky but comes together and holds its shape when you form it into a ball. Add more flour if necessary. Form it into an 8-inch round by pressing from the center out toward the edges, leaving a 1-inch border thicker than the rest. If the dough is too elastic, springing back rather than stretching when you try to shape it, don't fight it too much. Instead let it rest at room temperature for 15 minutes or so and try again.

4. Assemble the pizza. Have all the topping ingredients measured out and ready. Open the oven or broiler door, and quickly slide out the rack with the cooking surface (skillet, griddle pan, or baking stone) on it. Pick up the dough and quickly transfer it to the cooking surface, pressing it back into shape if need be, while being careful not to touch the cooking surface with your fingers. Quickly add the toppings to the pizza, following the order described in the recipe, then slide the broiler rack back in and close the door.

5. Broil the pizza. Broil until the crust has puffed up around the edges and darkened, preferably blackening in several spots, and the toppings are browned and any cheese melted, 3 to 4 minutes. If the top of the pizza starts to burn before the crust seems otherwise fully cooked, lower the broiler rack.

6. Remove the pan from the broiler, and use a peel to transfer the pizza from the pan to the countertop. Let it cool for a few minutes before cutting into quarters and eating.

MUSHROOM AND SPECK PIZZA

I came up with this pizza idea when sampling the beautifully made charcuterie of Nathan Anda, who sells at farmers' markets in the Washington, D.C., area. When he pulled out a package of fatty German-style speck and suggested that it would melt on top of pizza, I had to try it with a bagful of mushrooms I bought from a nearby vendor. He was right: The fat from the speck basted the mushrooms in richness. If you can't find German-style speck, substitute Italian lardo raw, thinly sliced bacon.

4 to 5 ounces mixed mushrooms, such as hen of
   the woods, oyster, and cremini, cut into halves or
   quarters if large
1 tablespoon extra-virgin olive oil
Kosher or sea salt
Freshly ground black pepper
All-purpose flour
1 (6-ounce) ball No-Knead Pizza Dough (page 104)
   or No-Knead Pizza Dough with Spelt (page 105)

2 tablespoons marinara sauce or crushed canned
   tomatoes (preferably San Marzano)
1 ounce Pecorino Romano cheese, freshly grated
1 ounce Parmigiano-Reggiano cheese, freshly
   grated
2 paper-thin slices Italian speck

If the dough has been refrigerated, transfer it to the countertop to let it rise for about 1 hour before making pizza.

Preheat the oven to 500°F.

In a large cast-iron skillet or on a flat griddle, toss the mushrooms with the oil, salt, and pepper. Transfer to the oven and roast for 10 to 15 minutes, until the mushrooms have collapsed and are nicely browned. Transfer the mushrooms to a plate.

Preheat the broiler with the rack set 5 inches from the element or flame. If you are using a cast-iron skillet or griddle pan for the pizza, set it over medium-high heat until it gets smoking hot, about 15 minutes. Transfer the skillet (turned upside down) or griddle pan to the broiler. If you are using a baking stone, heat it in a 500°F oven for an hour, then carefully transfer it to the broiler.

To shape the dough, dust a work surface liberally with flour and put the ball of dough on it. Sprinkle with flour and knead a few times until the dough comes together and holds its shape when you form it into a ball. Add more flour if necessary. Form it into an 8-inch

round by pressing from the center out toward the edges, leaving a 1-inch border thicker than the rest.

Make sure the topping ingredients are measured and ready before you assemble the pizza.

Open the oven or broiler door, and quickly slide out the rack with the cooking surface (skillet, griddle pan, or baking stone) on it. Pick up the dough and quickly transfer it to the cooking surface, pressing it back into shape if need be, while being careful not to touch the cooking surface with your fingers.

Spread a thin layer of the marinara sauce (to taste) on the pizza dough, leaving a 1-inch margin around the edges. Scatter the mushrooms (to taste) over the sauce, then sprinkle on the cheeses. Lay the slices of speck on top.

Broil the pizza for 3 to 5 minutes, until the crust has puffed up around the edges and blackened in spots.

Remove the pizza with a wooden or metal pizza peel or a thin square of cardboard, transfer it to a cutting board, and let it rest for a few minutes. Cut the pizza into quarters, transfer to a plate, and eat.

FIG, TALEGGIO, AND RADICCHIO PIZZA

When I asked friends for their favorite pizza-combination ideas, this one, from former *Boston Globe* Living Arts editor Fiona Lewis, jumped to the front of the line. First, I'm a freak for figs: fresh when they're in season, of course, but dried at other times of the year. Second, when Fiona mentioned it, I had just started yielding to an addiction to Taleggio, the pungent, slightly bitter Italian cheese that tastes of mushrooms. I immediately thought walnuts would be a perfect crunchy addition to this party, and I invited along my old friend radicchio to add even more bitterness. Once I got the layering order right (walnuts need to go on the bottom, under the nest of radicchio, to avoid burning under the broiler), this was a keeper. Obviously, if you want to make this when fresh figs are in season, by all means do so; skip the soaking-in-wine step and you'll be good to go.

3 dried Mission figs
½ cup dry red wine
2 tablespoons raw walnut pieces
All-purpose flour
1 (6-ounce) ball No-Knead Pizza Dough (page 104)
  or No-Knead Pizza Dough with Spelt (page 105)

2 tablespoons extra-virgin olive oil
½ small head radicchio, shredded (about ¼ cup)
2 ounces Taleggio or another pungent cheese,
  cut into small pieces

If the dough has been refrigerated, transfer it to the countertop to let it rise for about 1 hour before making pizza.

Preheat the broiler with the rack set 5 inches from the element or flame. If you are using a cast-iron skillet or griddle pan for the pizza, set it over medium-high heat until it gets smoking hot, about 15 minutes. Transfer the skillet (turned upside down) or griddle pan to the broiler. If you are using a baking stone, heat it in a 500°F oven for an hour, then carefully transfer it to the broiler.

Put the figs in a small skillet set over medium heat, pour in the wine, and bring to a boil. Turn off the heat and let the figs soak for at least 30 minutes. Drain, then chop into ½-inch pieces.

Toast the walnut pieces in a small, dry skillet over medium-high heat, shaking the skillet frequently, until they are very fragrant and starting to brown, 3 to 4 minutes. Immediately transfer to a plate, let cool, and then coarsely chop.

To shape the dough, dust a work surface liberally with flour and put the ball of dough on it. Sprinkle with flour and knead a few times until the dough comes together and holds its shape when you form it into a ball. Add more flour if necessary. Form it into an 8-inch round by pressing from the center out toward the edges, leaving a 1-inch border thicker than the rest.

Make sure you have all the topping ingredients measured out and ready before you assemble the pizza, because once you place the dough on the cooking surface you can't easily move it.

Open the oven or broiler door, and quickly slide out the rack with the cooking surface (skillet, griddle pan, or baking stone) on it. Pick up the dough and quickly transfer it to the cooking surface, pressing it back into shape if need be, while being careful not to touch the cooking surface with your fingers.

continued

FIG, TALEGGIO, and RADICCHIO PIZZA, continued

Drizzle 1 tablespoon of the oil onto the dough, scatter the walnut pieces on top, then the radicchio, then the chopped figs, and then the cheese. Slide the broiler rack back into the oven and close the door.

Broil the pizza until the crust has puffed up around the edges, the pizza has blackened in spots, and the cheese has melted, 3 to 4 minutes.

Remove the pizza with a wooden or metal pizza peel or a square of cardboard, transfer it to a cutting board, and let it rest for a few minutes. Drizzle the remaining 1 tablespoon of oil on top, cut the pizza into quarters, transfer it to a plate, and eat.

SMOKED TROUT, POTATO, AND FENNEL PIZZA

I'm such a purist about some things—I think all food people are. Tell me you're putting beans and tomatoes in chili, and the Texas boy in me bristles. But when one of my friends, an Israeli man of Norwegian heritage, came to a pizza-tasting party and—before he sampled it, I should note—declared this pizza combination "wrong, just wrong," why did it irritate me so much? Well, I suppose it's because I'm neither Norwegian nor Italian, so I couldn't understand why something so delicious could be anything but right. This combination was inspired by a pizza that friends told me I had to try from Coppi's Organic in Washington, D.C. I've taken shameless liberties with it.

1 small Yukon gold potato (about 4 ounces), cut into ¼-inch slices
2 tablespoons water
1 teaspoon extra-virgin olive oil
Kosher or sea salt
Freshly ground black pepper
All-purpose flour
1 (6-ounce) ball No-Knead Pizza Dough (page 104) or No-Knead Pizza Dough with Spelt (page 105)
2 tablespoons fresh whole-milk ricotta

2 ounces smoked trout, broken up into bite-size flakes
3 slices Herbed Lemon Confit (page 4) or substitute store-bought preserved lemon, coarsely chopped
¼ small fennel bulb, cut into paper-thin slices (about ¼ cup), plus a few fronds for garnish
1 tablespoon low-fat Greek-style yogurt, whisked until smooth

If the dough has been refrigerated, transfer it to the countertop to let it rise for about 1 hour before making pizza.

Preheat the oven to 500°F.

In a large cast-iron skillet, toss the potato slices with the water, oil, salt, and pepper. Cover the skillet tightly with aluminum foil and bake for 10 to 15 minutes, until the potatoes are soft but not browned. Transfer the potatoes to a plate.

Preheat the broiler with the rack set 5 inches from the element or flame. If you are using a cast-iron skillet or griddle pan for the pizza, set it over medium-high heat until it gets smoking hot, about 15 minutes. Transfer the skillet (turned upside down) or griddle pan to the broiler. If you are using a baking stone, heat it in a 500°F oven for an hour, then carefully transfer it to the broiler.

To shape the dough, dust a work surface liberally with flour and put the ball of dough on it. Sprinkle with flour and knead a few times until the dough comes together and holds its shape when you form it into a ball. Add more flour if necessary. Form it into an 8-inch round by pressing from the center out toward the edges, leaving a 1-inch border thicker than the rest.

Make sure you have all the topping ingredients measured out and ready before you assemble the pizza, because once you place the dough on the cooking surface you can't easily move it.

Open the oven or broiler door, quickly slide out the rack with the cooking surface (skillet, griddle pan, or baking stone) on it. Pick up the dough and quickly transfer it to the cooking surface, pressing it back into shape if need be, while being careful not to touch the cooking surface with your fingers.

continued

SMOKED TROUT, POTATO, and FENNEL PIZZA, continued

Layer the potato rounds on top of the dough, leaving the 1-inch margin bare, and plop dabs of ricotta here and there. Broil the pizza for 3 to 5 minutes, or until the crust has puffed up around the edges and blackened in spots.

Remove the pizza with a wooden or metal peel or a thin square of cardboard and transfer it to a cutting board. Scatter the trout, lemon confit, and fennel slices and fronds on top. Let the pizza rest for a few minutes. Drizzle it with the yogurt, cut it into quarters, transfer to a plate, and eat.

Layer the potato rounds on top of the dough, leaving the 1-inch margin bare, and plop dabs of ricotta here and there. Broil the pizza for 3 to 5 minutes, or until the crust has puffed up around the edges and blackened in spots.

Remove the pizza with a wooden or metal peel or a thin square of cardboard and transfer it to a cutting board. Scatter the trout, lemon confit, and fennel slices and fronds on top. Let the pizza rest for a few minutes. Drizzle it with the yogurt, cut it into quarters, transfer to a plate, and eat.

EGGPLANT AND SPICY HUMMUS FLATBREAD

To my mind, flatbread always calls out for eggplant or hummus, so why not eat the two together? I like to add to the complexity by frying up some extra chickpeas—something that, in greater quantities, makes for a fantastic party appetizer. Look for za'atar spice in Middle Eastern markets or buy it online from spice purveyors such as Penzeys.com.

¼ cup cooked chickpeas, preferably homemade (page 47), rinsed and drained
½ cup plus 1 tablespoon extra-virgin olive oil, plus more for brushing dough
1 teaspoon fleur de sel or other flaky sea salt
¼ teaspoon pimenton (smoked Spanish paprika)
1 small (5- to 6-ounce) Italian eggplant, cut into ¼-inch rounds

1 teaspoon za'atar spice (or substitute mixed Italian herbs)
1 (3-ounce) ball No-Knead Pizza Dough with Spelt (page 105), or one round of your favorite store-bought pita or other flatbread
½ cup Spicy Hummus (page 5)
¼ cup Citrus-Pickled Onions (page 19) (optional)

Preheat the broiler with the rack set 4 to 5 inches from the flame or element. Line a baking sheet with aluminum foil.

Spread the chickpeas on a paper towel on your countertop and lay another paper towel on top. Pat the chickpeas until very dry. Line a plate with paper towels.

Pour ½ cup of the oil into a small skillet over medium-high heat. When the oil starts to shimmer, scatter in the chickpeas, being careful to avoid splatters. Fry the chickpeas until they darken and become crispy, 5 to 6 minutes. Transfer them with a slotted spoon to the prepared plate. Immediately sprinkle them with ½ teaspoon of the salt and all of the pimenton. Strain the oil and save it for another use.

Lay the eggplant slices on the prepared baking sheet, drizzle with the remaining 1 tablespoon of oil, and sprinkle with the remaining ½ teaspoon of salt and all of the za'atar spice. Broil until browned and tender, 3 to 4 minutes, rotating the baking sheet if necessary to evenly cook the eggplant. Transfer to a plate to cool.

If you're making flatbread from the pizza dough, set the ball of dough in the middle of a piece of parchment at least 7 inches square or round. Press or stretch the dough into a 5- to 6-inch round, using a rolling pin if necessary. You want an evenly flat disk, so don't worry about trying to keep the edge thicker as with pizza.

Set a large cast-iron skillet fitted with a lid over high heat.

continued

Brush oil generously on top of the dough. Lift the parchment paper and dough carefully and flip the dough into the skillet so the oiled side is down. Quickly peel off the parchment from the top of the dough, and then brush the dough with oil, cover, and turn the heat down to medium.

After about 1 minute, remove the lid and use tongs or a large spatula to flip the disk over. It will have puffed up in places, darkened in others. Continue cooking, uncovered, for another minute or two, until the dough is spotted brown, puffy, and cooked through. Transfer to a plate. (If you're using pita or other store-bought flatbread, brush it with olive oil on both sides and heat it in the skillet, uncovered, for a minute or two on each side. Then transfer to a plate.)

Spread the hummus on one side of the flatbread, then lay the eggplant slices on top. Scatter the fried chickpeas and pickled onions over the eggplant, and fold the flatbread in half around the filling. Cut it into two pieces, and eat.

THREE-PEPPER PIZZA
WITH GOAT CHEESE

This is a pie that you can put together in a flash, because it depends on the idea that you've got some great condiments and accompaniments already made and just waiting for such a use as this. Like all my favorite pizzas, it depends on relatively spare but high-quality toppings.

All-purpose flour
1 (6-ounce) ball No-Knead Pizza Dough (page 104) or No-Knead Pizza Dough with Spelt (page 105)
¼ cup Red Pepper Chutney (page 17)
2 ounces soft goat cheese, cut into small pieces

5 or 6 pieces Pickled Anchos (page 20)
¼ cup loosely packed baby arugula leaves, stacked, rolled, and cut into strips
Extra-virgin olive oil, for drizzling

If the dough has been refrigerated, transfer it to the countertop to let it rise for about 1 hour before making pizza.

Preheat the broiler with the rack set 5 inches from the element or flame. If you are using a cast-iron skillet or griddle pan for the pizza, set it over medium-high heat until it gets smoking hot, about 15 minutes. Transfer the skillet (turned upside down) or griddle pan to the broiler. If you are using a baking stone, heat it in a 500°F oven for an hour, then carefully transfer it to the broiler.

To shape the dough, dust a work surface liberally with flour and put the ball of dough on it. Sprinkle with flour and knead a few times until the dough comes together and holds its shape when you form it into a ball. Add more flour if necessary. Form it into an 8-inch round by pressing from the center out toward the edges, leaving a 1-inch border thicker than the rest.

Make sure you have all the topping ingredients measured out and ready before you assemble the pizza, because once you place the dough on the cooking surface you can't easily move it.

Open the oven or broiler door, and quickly slide out the rack with the cooking surface (skillet, griddle pan, or baking stone) on it. Pick up the dough and quickly transfer it to the cooking surface, pressing it back into shape if need be, while being careful not to touch the cooking surface with your fingers.

Spread the red pepper chutney on top of the pizza dough, leaving a 1-inch margin. Scatter over the goat cheese pieces and pickled anchos.

Broil the pizza for 3 to 5 minutes, until the crust has puffed up around the edges and blackened in spots.

Remove the pizza with a wooden or metal peel or a square of cardboard, transfer it to a cutting board, and let it rest for a few minutes. Scatter the arugula on top, drizzle it with a little oil, cut it into quarters, transfer it to a plate, and eat.

CHAPTER 7
SANDWICHES

· ·

Sandwiches are among the most universally accessible and beloved homemade foods, possibly because in their most basic form they don't really require any cooking. Just stack, slice, serve. They're as easily eaten over the sink at midnight as they are at your desk at lunch or on the couch in front of the TV.

The only thing that makes them seem less than ideal is that pesky leftover-bread problem, but it's not much of a problem after all, because bread freezes so well (see page 120). So then you're left to worry about more important things, such as what you're going to put on your sandwich. Unlike my less-is-more mantra with pizza, a Dagwood-style approach is fine, as long as the ingredients are chosen carefully and work well together.

I apply some of the same principles that I use with tacos (which really are just tortilla sandwiches, aren't they?): Balance the richness with something tart and include something crunchy for a little textural variety.

HANDLING LEFTOVER BREAD

There are many, many recipes (even at least one cookbook) that can help you handle leftover bread, but it's really not all that complicated, thanks to the fact that bread freezes so well.

If you have a family of four, you can buy a loaf, cut it in half, and freeze half in one piece. But if you are a single cook, you may want only a slice or two at a time. Therefore I suggest that you reserve enough for four sandwiches (today and tomorrow, naturally), then slice the rest and freeze it in groups of two slices apiece in heavy-duty freezer-safe plastic bags. That way you can easily pull out just what you'll need for a sandwich, and the bread will thaw in only 15 to 20 minutes (or in about 30 seconds on High in the microwave). Thawed sliced bread is much improved by a little toasting.

I have two favorite ways to use leftover, even stale, bread:

- Make croutons. Cut the bread into cubes, toss with extra-virgin olive oil and salt, and bake at 425°F for about 10 to 12 minutes, turning the cubes over as necessary to keep the browning even. Once cooled, they will keep in an airtight container in a cool place for 1 to 2 weeks. Use them in soups (such as Fall Vegetable Soup with White Beans, page 58) or salads.

- Make bread crumbs. Follow the same procedure as for croutons, but omit the olive oil and salt, toasting the cubes until golden brown. Let them cool, then pulse them in a food processor to coarsely grind them. Bread crumbs can be stored in an airtight container for months in a cool place. Use them in Fideos with Sardines and Bread Crumbs (page 151).

PULLED PORK SANDWICH
WITH **GREEN MANGO SLAW**

Besides the Cochinita Pibil Tacos (page 95), this is the purest, least messed-with application of leftover Yucatan-Style Slow-Roasted Pork (page 66). In a riff on the North Carolina tradition of pork with a tangy coleslaw, I'm using green mango, which sounds exotic until you realize that it's just . . . green mango. Unripe, firm, not-yet-ready-for-prime-time mango. It's super sour, which is one of the reasons I like it. The other is that, depending on your supermarket, it might be even easier to find unripe mango than ripe mango. Of course, one turns into the other if you wait long enough.

Juice of 1 lime
2 teaspoons Asian fish sauce
2 teaspoons sugar
1 very firm, unripe (green) mango
2 shallot lobes, thinly sliced
12 large mint leaves, stacked, rolled, and thinly sliced
12 basil leaves (preferably Thai), stacked, rolled, and thinly sliced

½ cup packed fresh cilantro leaves, chopped
1 jalapeño chile, stemmed, seeded, and finely chopped
½ cup Yucatan-Style Slow-Roasted Pork (page 66), with 1 to 2 tablespoons additional reserved sauce from pan drippings
1 hamburger or other bun, halved and lightly toasted, if desired

In a medium bowl, stir together the lime juice, fish sauce, and sugar until the sugar is dissolved.

Use a Y-shaped vegetable peeler to peel the mango. Continue using the peeler to cut wide, very thin strips of flesh from the mango, working in as close to the pit as possible on all sides. Arrange the strips facing the same way and use a large knife to thinly slice them lengthwise. You should have about 2 cups of mango strips.

Toss the mango in the bowl with the lime juice mixture and add the shallots, mint, basil, cilantro, and jalapeño, tossing to combine thoroughly. Let rest for at least 30 minutes to let the flavors mingle.

Warm the pork by combining it with 1 tablespoon of the extra sauce and microwaving on Medium for 30 to 60 seconds, until it is hot, or put in a small saucepan over medium heat and cook, stirring

frequently, for 3 to 4 minutes. If desired, add another tablespoon of sauce so that the pork is very juicy and will soak into the bun.

To assemble the sandwich, place one of the bun halves on a plate. Pile on the pork, top with about ¼ cup of green mango slaw and the other bun half, and eat.

Note: This recipe makes about 2½ cups of slaw, more than you need for the sandwich, but it's a great side dish for simple grilled meats, and the flavor improves with a couple of days in the fridge. Or you can add steamed shrimp and baby spinach leaves to the leftovers and eat it as a lunch or dinner salad.

GINGERED CHICKEN SANDWICH
with AVOCADO and MANGO

The ginger packs a double-edged spicy punch in this sandwich, as fresh pieces in the chicken-poaching liquid and in powdered form in the avocado spread. Mango adds its sweet-tart, cooling magic.

2 slices challah or brioche (may substitute any soft sandwich bread)
2 cups water, plus more as needed
1 tablespoon kosher or coarse sea salt, plus more as needed
3-inch piece fresh ginger, peeled and finely chopped
1 small (about 4 ounces) boneless, skinless chicken breast half

½ teaspoon ground ginger
Juice of ½ lime
½ avocado, peeled and pitted
1 scallion, white and light-green parts, thinly sliced
Freshly ground black pepper
¼ to ½ mango, peeled and cut into ½-inch slices (about ½ cup)

Preheat the oven broiler with the broiler rack set 4 to 5 inches from the flame or element. Toast the bread on one side only, 1 to 2 minutes, until deep golden brown, being careful not to burn it. Transfer it to a plate.

Combine the water, salt, and ginger in a 1-quart saucepan over medium-high heat. Bring to a boil and add the chicken, making sure it is completely submerged; add more water, if necessary. When the water returns to a boil, turn off the heat. Cover and let the chicken sit for 20 minutes or until no trace of pink remains in the center. Remove and let cool.

While the chicken is cooling, combine the ground ginger and lime juice; stir until the spice has dissolved. Add the avocado and mash it with a fork; stir in the scallion and add salt and pepper to taste. Mix well.

Cut the chicken lengthwise into ½-inch slices and season it lightly with salt.

To assemble the sandwich, spread the avocado-ginger mixture onto the toasted side of one piece of bread. Layer the chicken slices on top, then the mango slices. Top with the other piece of bread, toasted side facing inward. Cut in half, and eat.

Note: If you can find only larger chicken breast halves, poach one that weighs up to 8 ounces (slice it in half horizontally before poaching), use half for this recipe, and save half for another use within a couple of days.

TUNA, EGG, AND POTATO SALAD SANDWICH

If you think this sounds something like a reconstructed salade Niçoise on bread, well, you'd be right, but the truth is, I got the idea in Italy, not France. On my first trip there, in Venice, I quickly became addicted to eating while standing up at one of the city's many bars. Besides *melanzana* (eggplant) pizza, my favorite dish was a sandwich that seemed the ultimate in decadence, because it consisted of potato salad on one side and tuna salad on the other. When I started making it for myself, it seemed only natural to combine both salads into one, and then to throw a hard-cooked egg in there (who doesn't like egg salad, after all?), along with a couple of olives for briny tartness.

2 thick slices rustic-style bread
1 egg
1 small new potato, cut into ½-inch cubes
1 (2.8-ounce) can top-quality imported Italian or Spanish solid tuna in olive oil
2 green olives, pitted and chopped
1 to 2 tablespoons mayonnaise
Kosher or sea salt
Freshly ground black pepper
4 or 5 baby spinach leaves, stacked, rolled, and thinly sliced

Halfway fill a medium bowl with cold water and add a cup of ice.

Preheat the oven broiler with the rack set 4 to 5 inches from the flame or element. Toast the bread under the broiler until deep golden brown on one side, 1 to 2 minutes. Transfer to a dinner plate.

In a small saucepan set over high heat, bring a quart of water to a boil. Using an egg pricker or a thumbtack, carefully poke a hole just through the egg shell on the rounder end. Use a slotted spoon to carefully lower the egg into the water, along with the potato cubes. As soon as the water returns to a boil, decrease the heat to medium-low or low so that the water is barely bubbling. Cook the egg and potato together for 8 minutes (for a slightly soft yolk in the very center) or 9 minutes for a fully cooked yolk.

Use a slotted spoon to transfer the egg and potato cubes to the bowl of ice water. When the egg is cool enough to handle, scoop it out and crack it all over against the countertop. Remove a piece of shell from the rounder end and return the egg to the water. After a minute or two, slip off the rest of the shell and transfer the egg to a cutting board. When it cools, coarsely chop it and transfer it to a medium mixing bowl. Scoop the potato pieces out of the water and transfer them to the bowl. Add the tuna, olives, and 1 tablespoon of the mayonnaise to the bowl and stir to combine, adding up to another tablespoon of mayonnaise if you want a creamier mixture. Lightly season with salt and pepper to taste.

To assemble the sandwich, sprinkle the spinach leaves onto the toasted side of one of the slices of bread, and top with the tuna-egg-potato salad and the other slice of bread, toasted side facing inward. Cut in half and eat.

PHILLY-STYLE CHICKEN CUTLET SANDWICH

One of my go-to sandwiches in Washington, D.C., is the chicken cutlet at Taylor Gourmet, where the owners hail from Philadelphia and the sandwiches are all homages to the way things are done in the City of Brotherly Love. Their sandwiches are studies in simplicity: not too many ingredients, but they're high-quality ones, treated well. I love their combination of crunchy chicken, bitter and spicy broccoli rabe, and slightly melting provolone. But at home I like to jazz things up by adding a mayonnaise spiked with peppadews, those miniature red peppers from South Africa that are pickled to sweet-and-sour perfection. If you can't find them, substitute your favorite bread-and-butter pickle.

3 tablespoons extra-virgin olive oil
½ teaspoon red pepper flakes
3 stalks broccoli rabe, cut into 2-inch pieces
4 or 5 peppadew peppers, drained and finely chopped
1 tablespoon mayonnaise
1 small (about 4 ounces) boneless, skinless chicken breast half

Kosher or sea salt
Freshly ground black pepper
1 egg
¼ cup Japanese-style panko
2 slices provolone cheese, preferably aged (piccante)
1 large soft Portuguese sweet roll or Philly-style submarine roll, halved

Pour 1 tablespoon of the oil into a medium skillet over medium heat. When it starts to shimmer, add the red pepper flakes and cook, stirring, for a minute or two. Add the broccoli rabe and sauté until the broccoli rabe is tender, 4 to 5 minutes. Use a slotted spoon to transfer the broccoli rabe and red pepper flakes to a plate or bowl.

In a small bowl, stir together the peppadew peppers and mayonnaise.

Lay the chicken between two large pieces of plastic wrap on your work surface, and pound it to a thickness of about ¼ inch. Season it generously on all sides with salt and pepper.

In a shallow bowl, whisk the egg to combine. Spread the panko crumbs onto a plate. Dip the chicken breast in the egg, then dredge it in the panko crumbs, turning it and patting them on with your hands to coat the chicken well.

Pour the remaining 2 tablespoons of oil into the skillet over medium heat. When it starts to shimmer, lay the chicken cutlet in the pan and let it cook undisturbed until it is golden brown on the bottom, 2 to 3 minutes. Use tongs to turn the cutlet over, then lay the provolone pieces on the cooked side of the chicken, overlapping slightly, and cook until the bottom is golden brown and the chicken is cooked through, 2 to 3 minutes. Transfer the chicken to a serving plate.

To assemble the sandwich, place the two roll halves on the serving plate. Spread one slice with the peppadew mayonnaise, then top with the chicken cutlet, broccoli rabe, and remaining roll half, and eat.

TUNA, CHICKPEA, AND ARUGULA SANDWICH

This is not the tuna sandwich of your childhood, but it hits all the right notes: richness from the oily tuna, starchy goodness from the chickpeas, bitterness from the arugula, a little tang from the artichoke hearts, and a hell of a tang from the Herbed Lemon Confit (page 5). If you don't have some of the latter in your refrigerator, store-bought preserved lemon slices will do.

2 thick slices rustic-style bread
1 (2.8-ounce) can top-quality imported Italian or Spanish solid tuna in olive oil
¼ cup cooked chickpeas, preferably homemade (page 47), rinsed and drained
Kosher or sea salt
Freshly ground black pepper

4 marinated artichoke hearts, drained and chopped
2 tablespoons packed baby arugula leaves, stacked, rolled, and thinly sliced
3 slices Herbed Lemon Confit (page 4), drained and chopped

Preheat the oven broiler with the rack set 4 to 5 inches away from the flame or element. Broil the bread until it is deep golden brown on just one side, 1 to 2 minutes, and transfer to a serving plate, toasted side up.

Drain the tuna, squeezing the oil out of it into a small bowl.

Toss the chickpeas into a small bowl and pour 2 teaspoons of oil from the tuna over them. Season with salt and pepper to taste, and use a fork to mash the chickpeas into the oil. If the mixture seems too dry for your taste, add a little of the marinade from the artichoke hearts.

To assemble the sandwich, spread the chickpeas onto the toasted side of one of the pieces of bread; top with the arugula, artichoke hearts, lemon confit, and tuna. Top with the other slice of bread, toasted side facing inward, gently press the sandwich with your hand, cut in half, and eat.

AVOCADO, SMOKED OYSTER, AND PISTACHIO BRUSCHETTA

Shortly after the first time I went to Cork Wine Bar, a bustling neighborhood restaurant a few blocks from me in Washington, D.C., I started making one of their signature appetizers for dinner parties. It's simply bruschetta with sliced avocado, crushed pistachios, a drizzle of pistachio oil, and a sprinkle of fleur de sel. It is rich and pretty perfect as an hors d'oeuvre. When I started making it for myself, it wasn't quite doing the trick. I wanted a little protein on there, as well as something to cut the richness. A can of one of my favorite products, smoked oysters, was the answer, as were tart green olives. I like to pump up the smokiness even further by tossing the oysters with a little smoked paprika, but I'll leave that up to you. With or without it, this appetizer has grown up into a meal.

2 tablespoons raw shelled pistachios
1 (3-ounce) can smoked oysters in olive oil, drained
¼ teaspoon pimenton (smoked Spanish paprika) (optional)

2 thick slices rustic-style bread
½ very ripe avocado, peeled and pitted
5 or 6 large green olives, pitted and chopped
Fleur de sel or other best-quality flaky sea salt

Heat the pistachios in a small, dry skillet over medium heat, shaking the pan frequently, until they are very fragrant and starting to brown in spots, 2 or 3 minutes. Immediately transfer them to a bowl to stop the cooking.

In a small bowl, toss the oysters with the pimenton.

Preheat the broiler with the rack set 4 to 5 inches from the flame or element. Broil the bread on one side until very dark brown, even slightly blackened in spots, 2 or 3 minutes. Transfer to a plate.

Divide the avocado flesh between the two bread slices and spread with a knife. Top with the oysters, then the green olives and pistachios. Sprinkle with a little salt, and eat.

SMOKED TROUT, GREEN APPLE, AND GOUDA SANDWICH

Some of my favorite sandwiches need very little prep work, just the right combination of top-notch ingredients. This is one of them. Dark bread, smoky fish, tart apple, and complex Gouda make magic together. All you have to do is slice, spread, cut, eat, and smile.

1 tablespoon mayonnaise
2 slices pumpernickel bread
2 ounces smoked trout, flaked with a fork
1 ounce aged Gouda cheese, cut into thin slices or crumbled

½ small to medium Granny Smith apple, cored and cut into ¼-inch slices
A few leaves baby arugula or baby spinach
Freshly ground black pepper

To assemble the sandwich, spread the mayonnaise on one side of both pieces of bread. Mound the trout on one of the bread slices, then top with the Gouda, the apple, and the arugula. Season with pepper. Top with the other slice of bread, cut in half, and eat.

CHAPTER 8
RICE, GRAINS, AND PASTA

. . . .

I could never be an Atkins diet spokesman, because I love my carbs too much. Over the years, like many other people, I've increased the presence of whole grains in my diet, but I haven't pushed white rice and pasta completely out of the way. How could I? Not when there's paella, fried rice, risotto, pappardelle, and spaghettini to make.

Pasta, rice, noodles, and all manner of grains are well suited to the solo cook because they keep so easily in the pantry, are easy to measure out for small quantities, and, particularly in the case of rice and grains, freeze so well once they're cooked, keeping their taste and texture when defrosted.

THAI FRIED RICE WITH RUNNY EGG

I'm a longtime fan of Jeffrey Alford and Naomi Duguid, cookbook authors who produce glorious books with a journalistic approach to food writing. Their stories and stunning photographs illuminate the culture behind the food of such places as Southeast Asia and lesser-known parts of China. They're also great fun to talk to, and when I interviewed them about their ways with fried rice (which they often make for themselves at home when one or the other is traveling), they insisted that for my own eating pleasure I make sure to always have nam pla prik in my refrigerator. This Thai condiment is simply fish sauce and chiles, which sounds like an almost lethally pungent combination, but when you make it, something magical happens. Each ingredient tames the other one, an effect that increases the longer the sauce sits in the refrigerator. This recipe is designed to use leftover rice, such as the stuff that comes in spades with Chinese takeout orders. Fresh rice doesn't work as well because it sticks. If you don't have a wok, you can use a nonstick skillet for this recipe, but it will take longer and won't be as much fun.

NAM PLA PRIK
½ cup Thai chiles
1 cup Asian fish sauce

FRIED RICE
1 tablespoon plus 1 teaspoon vegetable or peanut oil
4 cloves garlic, chopped
1 cup oyster or other mushrooms, cut into ½-inch pieces
1 cup cold cooked white or brown rice or farro (see page 143)

2 scallions, white and green parts, thinly sliced
1 tomato, cored and chopped (or substitute ½ cup canned crushed tomatoes)
2 teaspoons Asian fish sauce, plus more to taste
1 teaspoon low-sodium soy sauce, plus more to taste
1 egg
Kosher or sea salt and freshly ground pepper
Leaves from 10 to 12 cilantro sprigs (about 2 tablespoons) chopped
½ small cucumber, thinly sliced (about ¼ cup)
½ lime, cut into wedges

To make the nam pla prik, don food-safe gloves and stem the chiles, then thinly slice. (Alternatively, place the stemmed chiles in a food processor and pulse a few times, being careful not to puree them.) Transfer the chiles, including the seeds, to a glass container with a tight-fitting lid; add the fish sauce. Close tightly and refrigerate indefinitely. (The longer the mixture keeps, the more both ingredients will mellow. If desired, just replenish with more chile peppers or fish sauce whenever either gets low.)

To make the fried rice, remember to have everything measured out and ready before you start, because with high-heat stir-frying, everything happens pretty quickly. Heat a 14-inch flat-bottomed wok over high heat until a drop of water vaporizes within a second or two. Swirl in the 1 tablespoon of oil to coat the sides and bottom, then add the garlic and stir-fry until the garlic is just golden, about 20 seconds. Add the mushrooms and stir-fry until softened, 1 to 2 minutes. Resist the urge to turn down the heat, and keep everything moving.

Add the rice, breaking it up with your fingers as you toss it into the wok. Use a heatproof spatula to keep the rice moving for 2 to 3 minutes, scooping and tossing and pressing the rice against the bottom and sides of the wok to sear it. Add the scallions, tomato, fish sauce, and soy sauce. Stir-fry until the tomato breaks up and the scallions slightly soften, 30 seconds. Transfer the mixture to a dinner plate.

Wipe out the wok and decrease the heat to low. Pour the remaining 1 teaspoon oil into the wok. Break the egg into a small bowl, then carefully tip the egg from the bowl into the wok. Season with salt and pepper,

cover, and cook until the top of the egg has barely filmed over with white and the yolk is still runny, about 2 minutes. Carefully lift out the egg and place it atop the rice.

Garnish with the cilantro, cucumber slices, and wedges of lime, and eat it with as much nam pla prik as you wish, sprinkling it a teaspoon at a time onto the rice to taste along with squeezes of lime juice as you eat.

CORN RISOTTO WITH ROASTED CHERRY TOMATOES

Like so many other American cooks, I learned to make risotto from Marcella Hazan—not directly, of course, although wouldn't that be great? This is a quintessentially summertime recipe; make it when fresh corn, tomatoes, and basil are all converging on your local farmers' market or farmstand. Risotto is one of those dishes that makes great leftovers—especially to form into balls, stuff with cheese, roll in bread crumbs, and fry to make arancini. So if you like the thought of that in your future, feel free to double or triple this recipe. Eat this with a vibrant green salad and some chewy bread for a filling supper.

½ pint cherry tomatoes, stems removed
2 tablespoons extra-virgin olive oil
Salt and freshly ground black pepper
1 to 1½ cups Corn Broth (page 3) or vegetable stock
1 shallot lobe, coarsely chopped
1 clove garlic, coarsely chopped
Kernels from 1 ear fresh corn (about ¾ cup)

⅓ cup Arborio or other risotto rice
¼ cup dry white wine
2 teaspoons unsalted butter
2 tablespoons freshly grated Parmigiano-Reggiano cheese
2 or 3 large basil leaves, stacked, rolled, and thinly sliced

Preheat the oven to 400°F. Line a small roasting pan or baking sheet with aluminum foil.

Put the cherry tomatoes on the prepared pan and toss with 1 tablespoon of the oil and salt and pepper to taste. Roast for about 30 minutes, until the tomatoes collapse and brown slightly.

Meanwhile, in a small saucepan, bring the corn broth to a simmer over medium heat, turn down the heat to low, and cover.

Heat the remaining 1 tablespoon of oil in a small heavy saucepan over medium heat. When it shimmers, add the shallot and garlic and cook, stirring occasionally, until the vegetables are slightly soft, 3 to 4 minutes. Toss in the corn kernels and rice and cook, stirring quickly, until the rice grains are well coated, 1 to 2 minutes. Pour in the wine and

cook the rice, stirring frequently, until the liquid is almost gone, 5 minutes. Pour in ¼ cup of the hot corn broth and repeat, cooking and stirring, being sure to scrape the bottom of the pan when you stir so the rice doesn't stick. When the liquid is almost gone, add another ¼ cup of corn stock and continue cooking and stirring. Repeat until the rice has been cooking for about 20 minutes total. Taste to see if it is tender but al dente (still slightly firm to the bite inside the rice). Stir in the cherry tomatoes. Cook for another few minutes until the rice is tender but not mushy, adding a little more liquid to keep it very moist but not runny.

When the rice is done to your liking, add the butter and cheese. Stir to combine, taste, and add more salt if necessary. Transfer to a shallow bowl, top with the basil, and eat.

FRIED RICE WITH CAULIFLOWER AND KIMCHI

. . . .

The best thing about kimchi is this: It packs so much flavor and complexity, you can use it to make lightning-quick meals that taste as if they took hours to prepare. This fried rice, for instance, comes together in mere minutes. Cutting up the cauliflower might be the most time-consuming part. And yet this dish is downright addictive. If you don't have a wok, you can use a large nonstick skillet for this fried rice, but it will take a little longer to cook.

. . . .

1 tablespoon vegetable or peanut oil
½ small (5 to 6 ounces) cauliflower, cored and cut
   into ½-inch pieces
1 cup cold cooked white or brown rice or farro
   (see page 143)

½ cup Cabbage and Pear Kimchi (page 18), or your
   favorite store-bought kimchi, chopped
1 scallion, white and green parts, thinly sliced
Soy sauce

Remember to have everything measured out and ready before you start, because with high-heat stir-frying, everything happens pretty quickly.

Heat a 14-inch flat-bottomed wok over high heat until a drop of water vaporizes within a second or two. Swirl in the oil to coat the sides and bottom. Add the cauliflower and stir-fry until it softens and starts to brown, 3 to 4 minutes. Resist the urge to turn down the heat, and keep everything moving.

Add the rice, breaking it up with your fingers as you toss it into the wok. Use a heatproof spatula to keep the rice moving for 2 to 3 minutes, scooping and tossing and pressing the rice against the bottom and sides of the wok to sear it. Add the kimchi and scallion, and stir-fry until the kimchi heats through and the scallion softens, 30 to 60 seconds.

Season to taste with soy sauce, transfer to a dinner plate, and eat.

WOK FOR ONE

. . . .

You'd think a wok would be too big for single-serving meals, but you'd be wrong. I use mine for fried rice and wouldn't want to make it any other way. Even with smaller amounts, a regular-size wok (14 inches) provides the room you need to keep all the ingredients moving.

I don't have a wok ring on my stove, but these days you can buy woks that are flat on the very bottom but still have the bowl-like shape that allows such great tossing, scooping, and turning.

Buy a carbon-steel wok, not a nonstick one. The carbon steel conducts heat so efficiently that you can get the thing blazing hot, which is what you want for effective stir-frying. Once the wok is properly seasoned (I am a devotee of Grace Young's instructions in *The Breath of a Wok*), it will turn as slick as glass—much more nonstick than anything coated.

CURRIED BUTTERNUT SQUASH RISOTTO

This recipe was inspired by my discovery of single-serving-size butternut squash the size of hand weights at my local farmers' markets. Roasted butternut squash is a great thing to have on hand for use in various other dishes, though, so feel free to roast a larger one and use ½ cup of the flesh here, refrigerating the rest for up to a week or freezing for several months in an airtight container.

2 tablespoons shelled raw, unsalted pistachios
2 tablespoons unsweetened coconut flakes
1 small (8 ounces) butternut squash, cut in half, seeds removed
Kosher or sea salt
Freshly ground black pepper
2 teaspoons extra-virgin olive oil

About 2 cups low-sodium vegetable broth
½ teaspoon curry powder
1 large shallot lobe, coarsely chopped
1 plump clove garlic, coarsely chopped
⅓ cup Arborio or other risotto rice
1 teaspoon unsalted butter

Preheat the oven to 400°F. Line a small roasting pan with aluminum foil.

Set a small, dry skillet over medium heat and add the pistachios, toasting them while stirring or shaking the pan frequently, until they have browned evenly, 3 to 4 minutes. Immediately transfer them to a plate to cool, then coarsely chop.

Return the skillet to the stovetop over medium-low heat and add the coconut flakes. Toast them until they are light brown and fragrant, stirring often to prevent burning, 3 to 4 minutes. Immediately transfer them to a plate to cool.

Season the squash lightly with salt and pepper, and place it cut side up in the prepared roasting pan. Drizzle with 1 teaspoon of the oil. Roast for 35 to 40 minutes, until the squash is tender enough to be pierced easily with a fork. (Alternatively, microwave it on High, uncovered, for 4 to 6 minutes, until tender.) Let it cool, then scoop out the flesh and mash it with a fork; you should have about ½ cup.

Meanwhile, bring the broth to a boil in a small saucepan over medium-high heat. Decrease the heat to low and cover.

Heat the remaining 1 teaspoon of oil in a small, heavy saucepan over medium heat. Stir in the curry powder and cook until it is fragrant and sizzling, about 30 seconds. Add the shallot and garlic and cook, stirring occasionally, until they are slightly soft, 3 to 4 minutes. Toss in the rice and cook, stirring until the grains are evenly coated, 1 to 2 minutes. Pour in ¼ cup of the hot broth and cook the rice, stirring frequently, until the liquid is absorbed. Be sure to scrape the bottom of the pan frequently to keep the rice from sticking. Repeat with ¼-cup amounts, allowing the broth to be absorbed before the next addition; this will take about 20 minutes. You should end up using about 1½ to 1¾ cups of broth. The rice should be tender but al dente (still slightly firm to the bite inside the rice grain). Add the butternut squash. Cook for few minutes, until the rice is tender but not mushy, adding some of the remaining broth to keep the risotto moist but not soupy.

When the rice is done to your liking, stir in the butter, taste, and add salt if necessary. Transfer to a shallow bowl, sprinkle with the pistachios and coconut, and eat while the risotto is hot.

PERSONAL PAELLA WITH SQUID AND SCALLIONS

· ·

Ask my Catalan friend Pep and my Catalan-wannabe friend Ted which of the three of us makes the best paella, and prepare to hear much wailing and gnashing of teeth. Then you'll hear many excuses about exactly how and why I, neither having the privilege of a) growing up in Spain (Pep) nor b) having written a newspaper story about paella after interviewing the Spanish cooking authority Penelope Casas (Ted), managed to mop the floor with both of them in a paella cook-off when I lived in Boston several years ago. What can I say? The crowd was the judge, and the choice was clear. Of course, paella is a renowned dish for groups: In Spain, cooks will put a gargantuan paella pan over a huge fire to feed dozens. But with the right pan (I love my trusty steel crepe pan), it's easy enough to make for one, too.

· ·

1 cup seafood stock or clam juice
Small pinch of crumbled saffron
¼ teaspoon pimenton (smoked Spanish paprika)
4 to 5 ounces cleaned squid, bodies cut into
    ¼-inch rings and tentacles halved lengthwise
Kosher or sea salt
Freshly ground black pepper

2 teaspoons extra-virgin olive oil
⅛ teaspoon red pepper flakes, or more to taste
2 scallions, white and green parts, thinly sliced
2 cloves garlic, minced
⅓ cup Arborio, Bomba, or other short-grain rice
4 large cherry tomatoes, quartered

Preheat the oven to 400°F.

Combine the seafood stock, saffron, and pimenton in a small saucepan over medium heat and bring to a simmer; reduce the heat to very low and cover.

Lightly season the squid with salt and pepper. In an 8-inch cast-iron or other heavy skillet, heat 1 teaspoon of the olive oil over medium-high heat. When it shimmers, add the squid and cook, stirring frequently, just until the squid lose any translucence and exude their juices, 30 to 60 seconds. Transfer the squid to a plate and decrease the heat to medium.

Add the remaining 1 teaspoon of oil, then the red pepper flakes, scallions, and garlic and sauté until the scallion starts to soften, another 2 to 3 minutes. Add the rice and cook until the grains are well coated with the pan mixture, 1 minute.

Pour in the hot broth and bring to a gentle boil. Decrease the heat to medium-low. Taste the liquid

and add salt to taste, then let it continue to gently bubble, swirling the pan occasionally, for 8 to 10 minutes, or until the rice has swelled and absorbed much of the liquid; it should still be slightly soupy.

Stir in the squid and tomatoes. Transfer the pan to the oven and bake, uncovered, for 10 to 15 minutes, until the rice is al dente, or mostly tender but with a little resistance in the center.

Remove the pan from the oven, cover with a lid or aluminum foil, and let it sit for about 5 minutes, until the rice is tender. Uncover and return it to the stovetop over medium-high heat and cook for about 2 more minutes, to brown the bottom of the rice.

Spoon it out onto a plate, and eat. Don't worry if it sticks. Just scrape it up and know that this is what the Spanish call *soccarat*, the crispy pieces that are considered a sign of a great paella.

FAUX-LOGNESE WITH PAPPARDELLE

True Bolognese sauce takes hours to simmer and deepen. Since the Yucatan-Style Slow-Roasted Pork (page 66) is already deeply flavored from all those hours in the oven, all you need to do is take it on a brief trip to Italy. This makes a very hearty all-inclusive serving for one; you could easily stretch it to serve two by boiling up a little extra pasta and including a salad and some bread on the table.

2 ounces pappardelle or other wide noodles
1 tablespoon extra-virgin olive oil
1 slice pancetta, finely chopped (or substitute bacon)
1 shallot lobe, finely chopped
1 small carrot, finely chopped
1 small celery stalk, finely chopped
½ cup Yucatan-Style Slow-Roasted Pork (page 66), chopped

¼ cup dry white wine
¼ cup canned crushed tomatoes
2 to 3 tablespoons whole milk, plus more as needed
Kosher or sea salt
Freshly ground black pepper
Freshly grated Parmigiano-Reggiano cheese

Bring a 2-quart pot of salted water to a boil. Add the pasta, stir a few times to keep it from sticking, and cook according to the package instructions, until just al dente.

While the water is heating and the pasta is cooking, pour the olive oil into a medium heavy skillet over medium heat. When the oil starts to shimmer, add the pancetta, shallot, carrot, and celery and cook, stirring frequently, until it just starts to brown in spots, 6 to 8 minutes.

Add the pork, using a wooden spoon to stir it in and break it up as it cooks. Stir in the wine, cook for a minute or two until it is incorporated, then add the tomatoes and 2 tablespoons of the milk. Cook for another couple of minutes, and add more milk if

needed to keep the sauce loose. Taste and season with salt and pepper. Decrease the heat to low and cover to keep the sauce warm while the pasta finishes cooking.

When the pasta is ready, use tongs or a strainer to scoop it out of the water, holding it above the pot to drain off excess water, and plop it into the sauce in the pan. Toss it to combine, then transfer it to a bowl, sprinkle the cheese on top, and eat.

Note: If you don't have any leftover slow-roasted pork, you can substitute 4 ounces of raw ground pork. Brown it in the skillet before adding the bacon-and-vegetable mixture and proceed with the directions.

FARFALLE WITH CANTALOUPE AND PROSCIUTTO

The thought of this dish came to me when I saw new varieties of individually sized cantaloupes, about the size of grapefruits, at my local farmers' markets. As a single cook, I'm drawn to anything with that single-serving thing going for it. But if you can't find any of these little ones, use 1 cup of the flesh from a larger cantaloupe and save the rest for breakfast or a snack the next day. Now, I can imagine what you're thinking: pasta with cantaloupe? Seriously? I first read about it in Giuliano Hazan's *Thirty-Minute Pasta* and knew I had to downscale it—and add prosciutto, such a natural thing to pair with cantaloupe.

3 ounces dried farfalle (bow-tie) pasta
2 teaspoons extra-virgin olive oil
½ teaspoon red pepper flakes
1 slice prosciutto, cut crosswise into very thin strips
1 very ripe baby cantaloupe (about 10 ounces), peeled, seeded, and cut into ½-inch cubes (about 1 cup)

½ teaspoon tomato paste
1 tablespoon nonfat Greek-style yogurt
Kosher or sea salt
Freshly ground black pepper
Freshly grated Parmigiano-Reggiano cheese
3 to 4 large fresh basil leaves, stacked, rolled, and thinly sliced

Bring a 2-quart pot of salted water to a boil over high heat. Cook the pasta according to the package directions, until it is just al dente. Drain, reserving ½ cup of the cooking water.

Meanwhile, line a plate with a few layers of paper towels. Heat the oil in a small nonstick skillet over medium-high heat. Add the red pepper flakes and prosciutto; cook until the prosciutto is browned and crisp, about 5 minutes. Drain the prosciutto on the paper towel–lined plate.

Add the cantaloupe to the skillet and cook until it forms a chunky sauce, 4 to 6 minutes. Add the tomato paste, cook for 1 minute, then remove the skillet from the heat and add the yogurt, stirring to incorporate. Add the cooked pasta and toss to combine, adding some of the reserved pasta cooking water as needed if the sauce is too thick for your taste. Add salt and pepper to taste.

Transfer to a bowl, sprinkle with the cheese, basil, and reserved prosciutto, and eat.

FARRO SALAD WITH CHICKPEAS, CHERRIES, AND PECANS

My introduction to the joys of room-temperature farro salad came years ago in Boston, when I wrote an article about two chef-couples' different approaches to an outdoor dinner party. Gabriel Frasca and Amanda Lydon, who have since taken over the storied Straight Wharf restaurant on Nantucket to much acclaim, cooked the farro in the oven, then combined it with, among other things, fresh cherries, blanched and sautéed broccoli rabe, and pecans. Besides scaling it down to single-serving size, I stripped down their method considerably, standing in fresh arugula for the broccoli rabe so I don't have to cook it, adding protein in the form of chickpeas, and using dried cherries instead of fresh because I can get them year-round.

2 tablespoons raw unsalted pecans
1 cup cooked farro (see sidebar at left) (or substitute cooked white or brown rice or barley), cooled
⅓ cup cooked chickpeas, preferably homemade (page 47), rinsed and drained
½ cup lightly packed baby arugula leaves, coarsely chopped
¼ cup canned diced tomatoes and their juice

2 tablespoons unsweetened dried cherries
1 shallot lobe, finely chopped
6 large mint leaves, chopped
1 tablespoon extra-virgin olive oil
1 tablespoon red wine vinegar
Kosher or sea salt
Freshly ground black pepper

Toast the pecans in a small, dry skillet over medium-high heat, shaking the pan frequently, until they start to turn dark brown and smell very fragrant, 2 to 3 minutes. Immediately transfer them to a plate to cool.

In a medium bowl, combine the farro, chickpeas, arugula, tomatoes, cherries, pecans, shallot, and mint; toss to combine. Add the olive oil and red wine vinegar, toss, add salt and pepper to taste, and eat.

MAKING FARRO

I love the nutty flavor and slightly chewy texture of farro, the ancient wheat grain that's become popular in recent years, thanks to the ongoing influence of regional Italian cooking traditions in the United States. I also find it exceedingly easy and forgiving to cook. Some cooks suggest soaking it overnight and then cooking it like rice, but I find it easiest to simply boil it like pasta until it's as tender as you want, no soaking required.

You can find farro in health-food stores and stores with a good selection of traditional, imported Italian ingredients. Imported Italian farro typically comes in a 1-pound bag, often vacuum sealed. Here's how I like to cook it:

1. Bring a large pot of salted water to a boil.

2. Add the farro and continue boiling until the grains are mostly tender but still have a slight chewiness to them, 25 to 30 minutes. Drain in a fine-mesh colander and cool.

One pound of dried farro makes about 6 cups cooked, which you can refrigerate in an airtight container for up to 2 weeks. Just transfer it to the refrigerator to let it defrost overnight or all day before using.

CHARRED ASPARAGUS, TOFU, AND FARRO SALAD

Because I was so used to the watery texture and bland taste of regular tofu, the flavor and texture of marinated and baked tofu was a revelation: a little chewy and nicely tangy from the addition of soy sauce. I know you can make it yourself, but the store-bought kind is so easy to come by that I can't pass it up, especially because it improves even further with more cooking, such as broiling it along with asparagus to add crispness and color. This recipe is my concession to being outdoor space–challenged, meaning that instead of firing up my trusty Weber like I used to when I had a yard, I crank up the broiler to get a similar flame-kissed effect, without the smoke, of course. If you have a grill, by all means feel free to use a perforated grill pan or vegetable basket for the asparagus and tofu, cooking them until they get charred spots.

12 spears asparagus, woody ends trimmed
4 ounces store-bought baked tofu, preferably teriyaki-flavored, cut into ½-inch cubes
Kosher or sea salt
Freshly ground black pepper
1 tablespoon extra-virgin olive oil

1 cup cooked farro (see page 143) (or substitute cooked white or brown rice or barley), cooled
1 scallion, white and green parts, thinly sliced
1 teaspoon capers, drained
2 tablespoons Cashew Tamari Dressing (page 7), or more to taste

Preheat the broiler with the rack set 4 to 5 inches from the flame or element. Line a small baking sheet with aluminum foil.

Arrange the asparagus spears and tofu in a single layer on the prepared baking sheet. Season generously with salt and pepper, then drizzle with the oil. Broil for 6 to 8 minutes, until the asparagus and tofu have charred a deep brown, almost black, on one side. Remove and transfer to a plate to cool.

While the asparagus and tofu are cooling, combine the farro, scallion, and capers in a medium bowl. When the asparagus and tofu are cool enough to handle, chop the asparagus into bite-size pieces and add it, along with the tofu, to the farro mixture. Pour in the dressing and toss to combine. Taste, adjust the seasoning with more salt and/or dressing, if desired, and eat.

Note: If you don't have the Cashew Tamari Dressing (page 7) in the refrigerator, you can substitute 2 teaspoons tamari, 1 tablespoon olive oil, and 1 tablespoon chopped cashews.

MISO MAC AND CHEESE WITH MUSHROOMS

Miso is a common ingredient in vegan versions of cheesey recipes, because it helps make up for the sharp complexity that's missing without any dairy products. I love cheese too much to ever leave it out, so why choose? Combining the two together, and adding mushrooms, makes for a powerfully flavored dish that packs a punch of umami. This is a light dinner for one that you can bulk up with a salad.

1 teaspoon extra-virgin olive oil

2 ounces cremini, button, or other mushrooms, chopped (about 1 cup)

1 tablespoon unsalted butter

1 tablespoon all-purpose flour

¼ cup whole or low-fat milk

2 ounces sharp Cheddar cheese, grated (about ⅓ cup)

2 teaspoons white miso

2 ounces (about ¾ cup dry) elbow macaroni, cooked and drained

Freshly ground black pepper

3 tablespoons Japanese-style panko

Pour the oil into a small saucepan over medium heat. When it shimmers, add the mushrooms. Cook, stirring occasionally, until the mushrooms release their liquid and start to soften, about 5 minutes. Line a plate with paper towels, and use a slotted spoon to transfer the mushrooms to the plate. Pour off and discard the liquid and oil from the saucepan, and wipe it out.

In the same saucepan, melt the butter. When its foam subsides, whisk in the flour until smooth. Cook, stirring, until the mixture thickens a bit and the raw flour taste is gone, 2 to 3 minutes. Add the milk, cheese, and miso and stir until the cheese melts.

Add the macaroni and mushrooms, stir to thoroughly combine, and remove from the heat. Season generously with black pepper.

Preheat the broiler with the rack set 4 to 5 inches from the flame or element. Oil a small baking dish Transfer the macaroni mixture to the prepared baking dish and sprinkle the panko crumbs on top. Broil until the panko crumbs have browned, 1 to 2 minutes.

Remove from the broiler, let cool slightly, spoon onto a plate, and eat.

SPICY ALMOND SOBA NOODLES
WITH **EDAMAME**

This is one of my go-to vegetarian meals, probably because the almonds and almond butter (one of my addictions) helps me forget the dish is meatless. The combination of textures also helps make this dish satisfying, and the salad keeps well at room temperature, making it perfect for brown-bagging. The recipe scales up easily, and any leftovers can be refrigerated in an airtight container for up to 3 days. Almond butter is available at natural foods stores, many supermarkets, Whole Foods Market, and Trader Joe's.

2 ounces dried soba noodles
½ cup shelled edamame (fresh or frozen)
1 tablespoon sliced raw almonds
1 tablespoon almond butter (or substitute peanut or other nut butter)
2 teaspoons unseasoned rice vinegar, or more to taste

1 clove garlic, crushed and finely chopped
¼ teaspoon red pepper flakes, plus more to taste
2 tablespoons hot water, plus more as needed
Kosher or sea salt
1 scallion, white and green parts, thinly sliced
½ red bell pepper, stemmed, seeded, and thinly sliced

Bring a large pot of salted water to a boil over medium-high heat. Add the soba noodles and cook for 6 to 8 minutes, or according to package directions, until they are barely tender. Use tongs to transfer the cooked noodles to an individual-serving bowl, reserving the cooking water in the pot. Return the water to a boil over medium-high heat. Add the edamame and cook until tender, about 5 minutes. Drain and add to the noodles.

Meanwhile, toast the almonds in a small, dry skillet over medium-high heat, shaking the pan frequently, until lightly browned and smelling toasty, 2 to 3 minutes. Be careful not to let them burn. Immediately transfer to a plate to cool. When they have cooled, coarsely chop them.

To make the dressing, combine the almond butter, vinegar, garlic, and red pepper flakes in a small bowl. Add the hot water, stirring to mix well. If the dressing seems too thick, add more hot water, a teaspoon at a time, until it has reached the consistency you want. Add salt to taste; add more vinegar if you want the sauce tangier, and more red pepper flakes if you'd like it spicier.

Add the dressing to the noodles and edamame, along with the scallion, bell pepper, and chopped almonds. Toss to combine, adding more water if necessary, and eat.

FEDELINI WITH TUNA RAGU

My friend Domenica Marchetti knows her pasta. She's the author of several fantastic books on Italian cooking, but the latest, *The Glorious Pastas of Italy*, is probably the closest to her heart, so I had to ask her what kind of dish this mother and wife might make for herself on a night she's alone. She picked something that she grew up with, that her family made just once a year as part of the traditional Italian "feast of the seven fishes" on Christmas Eve. It dawned on her that she didn't need to wait for the holidays to make it, and now, neither do I. It's right up my alley. In fact, the day she sent me the recipe, I looked in my fridge and pantry to confirm I had every single ingredient on hand. I couldn't help but smile; dinner was sealed, deliciously.

1 (14.5-ounce) can diced tomatoes
1 large clove garlic, lightly crushed
2 teaspoons finely chopped fresh Italian flat-leaf
   parsley
1 tablespoon extra-virgin olive oil
1/8 teaspoon fine sea salt, or to taste
1/4 teaspoon red pepper flakes

1 (2.8-ounce) can top-quality imported Italian or
   Spanish solid tuna in olive oil, not drained
1 or 2 best-quality imported Italian or Spanish
   anchovy fillets in olive oil, coarsely chopped
1 teaspoon capers, drained and minced
3 ounces dried fedelini or cappellini (angel hair
   pasta)

Pour the tomatoes and their juices into a medium heavy saucepan and use a wooden spoon to mash them up a bit. Add the garlic, 1 teaspoon of the parsley, the olive oil, salt, and red pepper flakes. Turn the heat on to medium and bring to a simmer. Decrease the heat to medium-low and cook, stirring occasionally, until the tomatoes have thickened to a sauce consistency, about 20 minutes. (Reduce the heat to low if necessary to keep the sauce at a gentle simmer.)

Stir in the tuna, anchovies, capers, and the remaining 1 teaspoon of parsley. Cook until the sauce is heated through and the ingredients have all melded together nicely, another 3 to 5 minutes.

While the sauce is cooking, bring a pot of salted water to a boil. Add the pasta and stir to separate the noodles. Cook, according to the manufacturer's instructions, until al dente. Drain the pasta, reserving 1/2 cup of the cooking liquid.

Return the pasta to the pot and spoon some of the sauce over it. Toss well to thoroughly coat the noodles, adding a splash or two of the reserved cooking liquid if necessary to loosen the sauce. Transfer the pasta to a bowl, top with additional sauce, and eat.

Note: Any leftover sauce makes a delicious topping for bruschetta or crostini.

FIDEOS WITH SARDINES AND BREAD CRUMBS

· ·

When my Catalan friend Pep made me fideos, the Spanish dish that's much like a paella but with pasta instead of rice, the first thing I thought was: delicious. The second: What a great thing to make for one. You don't have to boil the pasta, the whole dish can be made in a single skillet, and you can scale it down easily. I like to make it with sardines because they last so long in my cupboard or refrigerator, they're considered one of the more eco-friendly fish in the world, and they give the pasta a salty, funky taste I love. This makes a hearty meal for one, but you can easily stretch it to serve two with a salad or another vegetable and bread on the side.

· ·

1¼ cups fish stock, clam juice, or water
1 plump clove garlic, thinly sliced
2 shallot lobes, thinly sliced
1 plum tomato, cored and chopped (or substitute 2 tablespoons canned crushed tomatoes)
½ small fennel bulb, cored and finely chopped
½ teaspoon fine sea salt
2 tablespoons extra-virgin olive oil

1½ tablespoons coarse dried bread crumbs, preferably homemade (page 120)
1 slice bacon, thinly sliced
3 ounces spaghettini, broken into 2-inch lengths (or substitute spaghetti or vermicelli)
½ (3.75-ounce) can sardines in olive oil, drained and chopped
Freshly ground black pepper

Preheat the broiler with the rack 4 to 5 inches from the flame or element.

In a small saucepan over medium-high heat, combine the fish stock, garlic, shallot, tomato, fennel, and salt, and bring to a boil. Decrease the heat to medium-low, cover, and simmer for about 10 minutes. Reduce the heat to very low and keep it hot.

Line a plate with paper towels. Pour 1 tablespoon of the olive oil into a small oven-safe skillet (that comes with a lid) over medium heat. When it starts to shimmer, add the bread crumbs and toast until golden brown, 1 or 2 minutes, watching carefully so they don't burn. Transfer the bread crumbs to the paper towel–lined plate, wipe out the skillet, and return it to the heat.

Pour the remaining 1 tablespoon of olive oil into the skillet. When it starts to shimmer, add the bacon and sauté until the bacon is browned and crispy, 2 to

3 minutes. Use a slotted spoon to transfer the bacon to the plate with the bread crumbs.

Toss the spaghettini pieces into the skillet and cook, tossing constantly with tongs, until they are toasted brown, mottled, and look like pretzel sticks, about 5 minutes. Pour in half of the hot fish stock, cover, and cook until it is almost absorbed, about 4 minutes. Add the remaining stock along with the vegetables, increase the heat to high, and cook uncovered, shaking the pan occasionally, until the mixture is only slightly soupy and the spaghettini pieces are slightly firmer than al dente, another 4 to 5 minutes.

Stir in the sardines, transfer the skillet to the broiler, and broil, watching carefully so it doesn't burn, until the fideos are darkly browned in spots on top and the liquid is absorbed, 1 to 2 minutes.

Scoop the fideos onto a plate, sprinkle the bacon pieces and bread crumbs on top, and eat.

CHAPTER 9
DESSERTS

· ·

Dessert is for company, and you can't be bothered, right? You've already made dinner for yourself—and there's just no way you're going to take time to make a sweet meal-ender, too.

I get it. As much as I love to bake, I have never once pulled out my pastry bag to pipe a rosette of whipped cream onto pie unless I'm serving it to friends. But that doesn't mean my sweet tooth deactivates when I'm cooking for myself. And that can be a dangerous thing. So when I have a dinner party, I pawn off cake or pie leftovers on departing guests and instead stock my fridge, freezer, and pantry with lighter ways to get my dessert fix: a yogurt parfait, for instance, or just some good fruit, nuts, and a little drizzle of honey.

There are times, though, when my need to actually bake (or, more accurately, eat something baked) gets the best of me. So I keep balls of cookie dough in my freezer, and bake off a few at a time when I need a fix. Or I use that modern baker's godsend, frozen all-butter puff pastry, as the base for a quick, individually sized fruit tart.

I do such things partly because that sweet tooth is aching and partly because, after a long day of work and a tasty dinner, I deserve dessert, too. Don't you?

NO-BAKE CHOCOLATE OAT COOKIES

Makes about 36 cookies

It wasn't until I moved to Washington, D.C., that it hit me why my mother always made the no-bake cookies some people call Raggedy Robins. It was the no-bake part she liked. During a West Texas summer, as in D.C., you definitely want to avoid any recipes that begin with the words "Preheat the oven," especially when you can get something so delicious without heat. I was compelled to tart these up a little bit, using higher-quality chocolate than we could get in West Texas in the 1970s and 1980s, deepening it further with instant espresso, and using almond butter instead of peanut. And I wanted to use rolled oats instead of the more highly processed instant ones. The result: an easy cookie—more of a confection than a cookie, honestly—that has grown-up kid appeal.

½ cup sliced raw almonds
6 ounces high-quality bittersweet chocolate
   (preferably at least 60% cacao), chopped
½ cup sugar
1 teaspoon instant espresso
6 tablespoons unsalted butter
½ cup whole milk

⅔ cup almond butter
1 teaspoon almond extract
3 cups rolled oats
½ cup unsweetened dried cherries, chopped
2 tablespoons fleur de sel or other flaky sea salt
¼ cup unsweetened cocoa powder

Line a baking sheet with parchment or waxed paper.

Toast the almonds in a small, dry skillet over medium-high heat, shaking the pan frequently, until lightly browned and smelling toasty, 2 to 3 minutes. Be careful not to let them burn. Immediately transfer to a plate to cool.

In a medium saucepan, combine the chocolate, sugar, instant espresso, butter, and milk and stir over medium heat until the chocolate and butter have melted and the mixture is smooth. Stir in the almond butter and almond extract until smooth, then stir in the oats. Cook, stirring frequently, until the oats are slightly softened, 3 to 5 minutes. Remove from the heat and stir in the cherries and almonds, mixing well to combine.

Let cool slightly, then scoop out the dough by the rounded tablespoon and drop onto the parchment-lined baking sheet. (Don't worry about spacing them far apart; since they aren't baked, they won't spread.) Sprinkle the cookies with the sea salt, then sift cocoa powder generously over the tops.

Transfer the baking sheet to the refrigerator and chill the cookies for at least 1 hour, until they have firmed up. Store in an airtight container in the refrigerator for up to 2 weeks, or in the freezer for several months.

CARDAMOM–BROWN SUGAR SNICKERDOODLES

Makes about 70 cookies

• •

I know I'm not alone when I say that snickerdoodles were my favorite cookie as a kid. Hell, they're pretty much my favorite cookie as an adult. My mother's 1970s recipe used shortening, but I prefer to make them with all butter, to deepen their flavor with brown sugar, and to scent them heavily with ethereal cardamom. This recipe calls for them to cool on a wire rack, but do yourself a favor and eat at least a few while they're still warm, and be prepared to go weak-kneed. Snickerdoodles will keep at room temperature, in an airtight container, for about 3 days.

• •

2¾ cups all-purpose flour
2 teaspoons cream of tartar
1 teaspoon baking soda
1½ teaspoons ground cardamom
¼ teaspoon salt

1 cup unsalted butter, at room temperature
1½ cups packed light brown sugar
2 eggs
1 teaspoon vanilla extract
¼ cup granulated sugar

In a large bowl, sift together the flour, cream of tartar, baking soda, 1 teaspoon of the cardamom, and salt.

Combine the butter and brown sugar in the bowl of a stand mixer fitted with the paddle attachment. Beat on medium speed for 1 minute. Turn the speed to high and beat until very light and fluffy, 2 or 3 minutes, stopping a couple of times to scrape down the sides of the bowl as needed. Decrease the speed to medium and beat in the eggs, one at a time, and the vanilla.

Turn off the mixer. Add about one-third of the dry ingredients to the mixer bowl, and beat on low speed until fully incorporated. Repeat two more times, stopping to scrape down the sides of the bowl as needed, until the dry ingredients are incorporated.

Transfer the dough to the refrigerator and chill for about an hour, until firm.

In a medium bowl, stir together the granulated sugar and remaining ½ teaspoon of cardamom. Use a #100 disher (a ¾-tablespoon scoop) or a tablespoon to scoop small balls of dough a few at a time into the

sugar-cardamom mixture, then roll the pieces to coat them and lightly roll them into balls between your palms, pressing the sugar mixture into the dough.

Preheat the oven to 350°F with the oven rack in the middle of the oven. Line a baking sheet with parchment paper.

Set as many of the cookies as you intend to bake about 2 inches apart on the prepared baking sheet. Bake for 5 minutes, then rotate the baking sheet front to back. Continue baking for another 4 to 6 minutes, until the tops of the cookies are crackled and the edges are just barely browned. Transfer to a wire rack to cool.

Set the remaining dough close together but without touching on a baking sheet and freeze until firm, at least 1 hour. Remove the baking sheet from the freezer and put the cookies in a freezer-safe heavy-duty resealable plastic bag, rolling out the excess air before you seal it. Return to the freezer and store for up to 3 months. Bake the frozen cookies for 14 to 16 minutes, until the tops of the cookies are crackled and the edges are just barely browned.

PISTACHIO BUTTER COOKIES

Makes about 24 small cookies

• •

Why wouldn't you bake cookies for yourself? Cookie dough freezes beautifully, and if you cut it into portions before freezing, you can have a plastic bag filled with the potential for cookies any time you feel like it. These salty-sweet cookies use one of my go-to ingredients: homemade nut butter. I use a Vita-Mix to churn just about any freshly roasted nut into butter, but you can accomplish the same trick with a food processor and a little oil. A food processor nut butter won't be as super-smooth as one made in a Vita-Mix, but in a cookie like this, a little sandy texture from the bits of ground pistachio is a good thing.

• •

¾ cup shelled, roasted, and salted pistachios
1 to 2 tablespoons vegetable oil
4 tablespoons unsalted butter, at room
    temperature
½ cup packed light brown sugar

1 egg yolk, at room temperature
½ teaspoon vanilla extract
⅔ cup all-purpose flour
¼ teaspoon baking soda

Pour ½ cup of the pistachios into a food processor and process until finely ground. With the motor running, start pouring in 1 tablespoon of the vegetable oil in a thin stream through the food processor's opening, stopping when the ground pistachios turn into a paste, and adding more oil if needed. Scrape the pistachio butter into a bowl.

Coarsely chop the remaining ¼ cup of pistachios.

With an electric stand mixer fitted with the paddle attachment or a hand mixer, beat the butter and brown sugar on medium speed until incorporated. Beat on high spread until very smooth, 1 to 2 minutes. On medium speed, beat in the egg yolk and vanilla until well blended, scraping down the sides of the bowl if necessary. Beat in the pistachio butter until thoroughly blended.

In a medium mixing bowl, whisk together the flour and baking soda. With the electric mixer on low speed, slowly add the dry ingredients to the pistachio butter mixture until there are no patches of flour. Add the chopped pistachios and mix until thoroughly combined.

Divide the dough in two. Transfer half the cookie dough to a large sheet of plastic wrap on your work surface and form it into a 7-inch log, using the plastic wrap to help roll and shape it. Wrap it in plastic wrap, twist the ends, and refrigerate for 30 minutes, or until firm. Repeat with the other half of the dough.

Preheat the oven to 350°F. Line a baking sheet with parchment paper, and position a rack in the middle of the oven.

When the logs are firm, set them back on your work surface, and use a sharp knife to cut the dough into ½-inch pieces. (You should have about two dozen.) Set as many of the cookies as you intend to bake about 2 inches apart on the prepared baking sheet.

Bake for 12 to 15 minutes, rotating the baking sheet front to back halfway through cooking, until they are lightly golden and the edges have started to darken.

Remove from the oven and let the cookies cool for a few minutes on the baking sheet, then transfer to a rack to finish cooling.

Put the remaining cookies on a second baking sheet and transfer it to the freezer.

Freeze the cookies for at least an hour, until they are hard. Remove the baking sheet from the freezer and put the cookies in a freezer-safe heavy-duty resealable plastic bag, rolling out the excess air before you seal it. Return to the freezer and store for up to 3 months. Bake the frozen cookies for 15 to 20 minutes, until lightly golden.

CAPPUCCINO TAPIOCA PUDDING
WITH CARDAMOM BRÛLÉE

Makes 6 (½-cup) servings

· ·

There's really nothing quite like tapioca pudding to take me back to childhood, when I would eat those plastic cups of the store-bought variety. Of course, homemade is so much better, and it's really not difficult to make. It just requires a little patience and some stirring. I like to make a few cups at a time, eat one (or, okay, two or three). Then, before things get really out of control, I portion the rest into ½-cup ramekins and store them in the freezer. To take it over the top, I sprinkle just a touch of one of my favorite aromatic spices, cardamom, on top, along with some sugar, and torch the top to get that crackly brûléed effect.

· ·

3 cups milk, preferably low-fat
⅓ cup small pearl tapioca
1 tablespoon instant espresso powder
2 egg yolks, whisked to combine

¼ teaspoon fine sea salt
⅓ cup plus 2 tablespoons sugar
½ teaspoon ground cardamom

Pour 1 cup of the milk into a heavy saucepan. Add the tapioca and let soak for at least 30 minutes.

Pour the remaining 2 cups of milk into a mixing bowl or glass measuring cup, sprinkle the espresso powder over, let it sit for a minute or two, and then stir to dissolve.

Whisk the espresso-milk mixture into the tapioca mixture, along with the egg yolks, salt, and ⅓ cup of the sugar. Over medium heat, slowly bring the mixture just barely to a boil, stirring constantly; it will take 10 to 15 minutes. Reduce the heat until the mixture is barely simmering, and continue cooking the tapioca, stirring occasionally, until the beads swell up and become almost translucent and the custard thickens, another 15 to 20 minutes.

Remove from the heat and let it cool. Spoon the pudding into 6 individual ½-cup ramekins and wrap each in plastic wrap, pressing the plastic directly onto the surface of the pudding to prevent a skin from forming. Refrigerate until chilled. It will keep it the refrigerator for several days or in the freezer for up to 2 months.

When you are ready to eat, unwrap one of the ramekins of pudding (thaw it first if frozen), and sprinkle the top with 1 teaspoon of the remaining sugar and a pinch of cardamom. Use a small culinary blowtorch to caramelize the sugar on top, keeping the torch moving so you deeply brown but don't blacken the sugar, then eat.

HIBISCUS-POACHED PEACH

. . . .

I stumbled across this idea when I was making one of my regular summertime batches of hibiscus tea, while also wishing that the peaches in a paper bag on my countertop would hurry up and ripen already. I peeled a peach, let it steep in the hot tea for a while, and there you have it. Not only did the peach soften, but it also took on the loveliest color from the hibiscus, not to mention that addictive flowery tang. I later gilded the lily by boiling down a little more of the tea to make a glaze. The best part: I still had my tea, which I later cut with sparkling water and spiked with tequila.

. . . .

1 not-quite-ripe peach, preferably a freestone (not cling) variety
2 cups water
¼ cup dried hibiscus flowers

¼ cup sugar
2 tablespoons low-fat Greek-style yogurt, whisked smooth

Peel the peach with a serrated vegetable peeler if you have one. If you don't, pour the water into a small saucepan and bring it to a boil. Cut a shallow X shape on the bottom of the peach, and immerse it in the water for about 1 minute, then remove it with a slotted spoon and decrease the heat so that the water is at a bare simmer. Let the peach cool; peel the skin off, starting where it has curled up around the X shape. Cut the peach in half and remove the pit. (If you are able to peel the peach with a peeler, bring the water to a boil and then reduce to a bare simmer.)

Add the hibiscus and sugar to the water and stir to dissolve the sugar. Cook the hibiscus for about 5 minutes, until the water is a deep burgundy color. Immerse the peach halves, turn off the heat, and cover the saucepan. Let the peach sit in the hibiscus

tea for at least 30 minutes, until it is stained red. Use a slotted spoon to transfer the peach halves to a dessert bowl.

Reserve about ¼ cup of the hibiscus tea and one of the rehydrated hibiscus flowers. Strain the rest of the tea, transfer it to a pitcher, and refrigerate it for drinking; discard the flowers.

Pour the reserved hibiscus tea into a wide skillet set over medium-high heat. Bring it to a boil and let it bubble away until it reduces to a syrupy glaze, 5 to 10 minutes.

Pour the glaze over the peach halves, garnish with the reserve hibiscus flower, drizzle with the Greek yogurt, and eat.

SPICY COCONUT SORBET

Makes 4 servings

· ·

Why does coconut sorbet taste so rich, even without cream or eggs? Well, because there's plenty of fat in the coconut milk itself. It's one of the easiest sorbets in the world to make, thanks to the prevalence of decent canned coconut milk, but I like to give it a spark of heat, too. Eat this on its own, or with a cookie or other dessert of your choice. It goes especially well with chocolate. Remember that to make good ice cream with a machine that requires a prefrozen canister, you need to plan ahead and put the canister in the freezer at least 2 days before you're going to make the ice cream. (I store mine there.)

· ·

2 (13- to 14-ounce) cans coconut milk, shaken well
    before opening
½ cup packed dark brown sugar

2 Thai chiles, slit open
1 tablespoon tequila

Pour the coconut milk into a medium saucepan over medium-high heat and stir in the brown sugar. Bring the mixture to a boil, decrease the heat to low so that it is barely simmering, and cook, stirring occasionally, until the brown sugar is fully melted and the coconut milk is smooth, 3 to 4 minutes. Add the chiles, cover, and remove from the heat. Let steep for an hour.

Pour the coconut milk into a bowl and let cool to room temperature. Stir in the tequila. Cover with plastic wrap, transfer to the refrigerator, and let it thoroughly chill for several hours, preferably overnight.

Once the mixture is very cold, fish out the chiles, then taste. If the sorbet base isn't spicy enough for you, open up one of the chiles, scrape in a few of the seeds, and stir to combine. Transfer the cold sorbet base to an ice-cream maker and process according to the manufacturer's instructions. The sorbet can be stored frozen, covered in an airtight container, for a few weeks.

YOGURT PARFAIT WITH RHUBARB-GINGER SAUCE AND STRAWBERRIES

This is an easy, off-the-cuff dessert with plenty of options and jumping-off points. If you want something richer, feel free to use higher-fat yogurt. I pair the rhubarb with strawberries because the two have overlapping seasons and are such stunning partners, but if you've got access to other good fruit, this parfait also works beautifully with blackberries, raspberries, blueberries—even winter citrus, such as neat slices of Cara Cara or blood oranges, clementines, or tangerines.

6 or 7 large rhubarb stalks, trimmed and cut into ¼-inch slices (about 4 cups)
2-inch piece fresh ginger, peeled and minced (about 2 tablespoons)
½ cup sugar
⅓ cup water
¼ cup ripe, in-season strawberries
4 large mint leaves, stacked, rolled, and thinly sliced
½ cup fat-free or low-fat Greek-style yogurt

Combine the rhubarb, ginger, sugar, and water in a medium saucepan over medium-high heat and bring to a boil. Decrease the heat to a simmer, cover, and cook until the rhubarb and ginger are tender, about 10 minutes. Uncover, increase the heat to medium-high, and let the mixture bubble away until it has slightly reduced and thickened, 3 to 4 minutes. Remove from the heat and let cool. Reserve ¼ cup for the parfait and refrigerate the remaining 1¾ cups in an airtight container for up to 2 weeks or freeze it for several months.

When you are ready to eat, drop a few strawberries in the bottom of a large-bowled wineglass or champagne flute and sprinkle with a little mint. Add a tablespoon of cooled rhubarb-ginger sauce and 2 to 3 tablespoons of yogurt. Repeat a few times, ending with strawberries and mint.

Note: The recipe makes about 2 cups of rhubarb-ginger sauce, enough for 8 servings of parfait. You can refrigerate it for up to 2 weeks or freeze it for months.

YOGURT PARFAIT WITH MULLED RED WINE SYRUP, ORANGES, AND ALMONDS

Another parfait idea, using the same principle and base (Greek-style yogurt) but different accompanying layers. Feel free to use higher-fat yogurt if desired. I like to use Cara Cara oranges, those vibrant pink-fleshed ones, but blood oranges are deliciously striking here, and regular navel oranges or ruby red grapefruit are no slouches, either.

2 tablespoons sliced almonds
1 Cara Cara orange
¼ cup Mulled Wine Syrup (page 6), made with red wine

½ cup fat-free or low-fat Greek-style yogurt

Toast the almond slices in a small dry skillet over medium-high heat, stirring constantly, until they are lightly browned and begin to smell toasty, 2 to 3 minutes. Watch carefully; nuts can burn quickly. Transfer to a dish to cool.

Use a chef's knife to slice off both ends of the orange. Stand the orange on one end, hold it steady with one hand, and slice from the top edge downward along the curve of the fruit, cutting away both the peel and the pith but leaving as much of the flesh as possible. Working over a bowl to catch the juices, hold the orange in one hand and use a paring knife in the other to cut between the sections, detaching each section of fruit from its surrounding membrane. Let the sections fall into the bowl as you work.

Drop a few orange sections into the bottom of a large-bowled wineglass or champagne flute. Drizzle with a tablespoon of red wine syrup and top with a few almonds and then 2 or 3 tablespoons of yogurt. Repeat several times until the ingredients are used up, ending with oranges, syrup, and almonds on top if possible, and eat.

COCONUT FRENCH TOAST
WITH **BANANAS FOSTER**

I placed this dish in the dessert chapter, but it's so filling it might be best thought of as a brunch dish, or perhaps dessert-for-dinner. Adding sweetened bread crumbs to the preparation makes a French toast with extra crunch and a dark exterior, a nice contrast to the light, moist interior. I've turned the French custard toward the tropics by using coconut milk, and taken the topping to New Orleans with the classic combination of bananas, butter, rum, and pecans. Any other seasonal fruit can work: sliced apples or peaches sautéed in butter, fresh berries, or, when the fruit bowl is empty, your favorite jam.

3 tablespoons pecan halves
1 egg
¼ cup coconut milk
¼ teaspoon vanilla extract
1 thick (¾- to 1-inch) slice rich white bread, such as brioche or challah, trimmed neatly into a round or square (crusts removed)
¼ cup Japanese-style panko

2 tablespoons dried unsweetened coconut flakes (medium shred)
1 teaspoon granulated sugar
1 tablespoon plus 1 teaspoon unsalted butter
1 teaspoon dark brown sugar
1 banana, peeled and diagonally sliced ½ inch thick
2 tablespoons dark rum

Toast the pecans in a small, dry skillet over medium-high heat, shaking the pan frequently, until they start to turn dark brown and smell very fragrant, 2 to 3 minutes. Immediately transfer them to a plate to cool.

Whisk the egg, coconut milk, and vanilla extract together in a shallow bowl. Add the bread; let it stand for about 10 minutes, turning it over about halfway through, until it has absorbed most of the liquid.

Combine the panko crumbs, coconut, and granulated sugar on a plate. Use a spatula to transfer the soaked bread to the crumb mixture, and turn to coat both sides evenly. Pat as much of the mixture as you can onto the bread.

Melt 1 tablespoon of the butter over medium-low heat in a small skillet. Add the bread and cook until it is golden brown and crusted, 3 to 4 minutes. Turn it over and cook another few minutes, until it is golden brown on the second side. (Reduce the temperature

as needed to keep the bread from getting too dark.) Transfer to a plate. The inside of the French toast will be fairly spongy.

Add the remaining 1 teaspoon of butter to the pan and let it melt. Add the brown sugar and stir until it melts, 1 to 2 minutes. Add the banana slices and stir until they are warmed through and coated with the butter in the pan, 1 minute. Add the pecans and rum, and stir to combine.

Spoon the warmed banana mixture over the French toast, and eat.

Note: Some brands of coconut milk, such as Chaokoh from Thailand, are available in 5.6-ounce cans rather than the standard 13.5 to 14 ounces. Store coconut milk in the refrigerator for up to 1 week, or freeze in ice-cube trays and then store the cubes in freezer-safe heavy-duty plastic bags for several months.

CHERRY-ALMOND TART

. . . .

Puff pastry is a boon for the solo cook. You can keep it frozen, then defrost and cut off enough for just one serving, refreezing the rest. I've been known to make my own puff pastry, but Dufour makes such high-quality, all-butter dough that I rarely get my hands dirty with the homemade stuff anymore. (It's available in many parts of the country, but is not as widely available as puff pastry by Pepperidge Farm, which I like less because it uses shortening.) Now in the middle of winter, when the memory of fresh cherries and other pie fruit is a distant memory, I can combine dried cherries, almonds, and Mulled Wine Syrup (page 6) on a simple piece of puff pastry and bake up a tart that seems like the essence of summer.

. . . .

1 (4 by 4-inch) square frozen store-bought puff pastry, preferably all-butter (such as Dufour brand), defrosted

3 tablespoons unsweetened dried cherries

3 teaspoons Mulled Wine Syrup (page 6), made with red wine

2 tablespoons sliced almonds

2 tablespoons low-fat Greek-style yogurt, whisked smooth

Preheat the oven to 400°F. Line a baking sheet with parchment paper.

On a lightly floured countertop, roll out the puff pastry to about 6 inches square. Pierce the dough every ½ inch with a fork; this helps the pastry rise more evenly. Mound the cherries in the center of the dough and drizzle 2 teaspoons of the red wine syrup over them (but not the pastry). Lightly moisten the edges of the dough with water, pull it up, and fold it over to the edges of the cherries, forming pleats so that it cradles the fruit. Scatter the almonds on top.

Transfer the tart to the prepared baking sheet and bake for 20 to 25 minutes, until the pastry has puffed and turned golden brown. Remove it from the oven and let cool for a few minutes. Transfer to a dessert plate, drizzle with the remaining 1 teaspoon of red wine syrup, spoon on a dollop of yogurt, and eat.

BLUEBERRY-LEMON TART
WITH **TOASTED COCONUT**

All you really need for a good dessert is some good jam and a little pastry in your freezer. This follows the same principle as the Cherry Almond Tart (page 163), but makes use of Blueberry Lemon Jam (page 10). You can substitute another homemade or store-bought jam of your choice.

1 (4 by 4-inch) square frozen store-bought puff pastry, preferably all-butter (such as Dufour brand), defrosted
¼ cup Blueberry Lemon Jam (page 10)

2 tablespoons unsweetened, large coconut flakes
2 tablespoons low-fat Greek-style yogurt, whisked smooth

Preheat the oven to 400°F. Line a baking sheet with parchment paper.

On a lightly floured countertop, roll out the pastry to about 6 inches square. Pierce the dough every ½ inch with a fork; this helps the pastry rise evenly. Mound the jam in the center of the dough. Lightly moisten the edges of the dough with water and pull and fold up the sides to the edges of the jam, forming pleats so the dough cradles the jam. Scatter the coconut flakes on top.

Transfer the tart to the prepared baking sheet and bake for 20 to 25 minutes, until it has puffed and turned golden brown. Remove from the oven and let cool for a few minutes.

Transfer to a dessert plate, spoon on the dollop of yogurt, and eat.

COOKING FOR TWO

Culinary seduction is the stuff of novels and movies, but it hasn't been part of my story, at least not yet. As much as I've imagined possessing the power of that woman in *Like Water for Chocolate* to ignite the (quite literal) fires of passion with my cooking, in my dating life so far home-cooked food has mostly been a matter of comedy, a point of control, or, frankly, the source of some regret.

Note to self, or perhaps to self's therapist: Could that be why I'm single?

I don't remember ever cooking for my first great love, because when I met him I was living in a cooperative apartment building in Austin while going to the University of Texas. It was like a dormitory but with one very important exception: The residents do all the work, and make all the decisions. Meals were included—prepared by, of course, teams of students. We could bring guests to dinner, for a price, but Charlie and I, well, we needed our privacy.

Within weeks, we had moved in together and were doing the penniless-Austin-slacker thing. I would've been making him ramen noodles and canned beans with rice, except he brought home the bacon—or, more accurately, Church's fried chicken, where he worked as a manager. Every night for most of a year, we ate the better part of a family box (never a "bucket," I learned, which is from that other chicken place).

When the relationship derailed, it was a train wreck of near-gothic proportions, or at least that's how it felt to a nineteen-year-old. I'd like to think the collapse had something to do with all that chicken—a carb, protein, and fat overload?—because the truth, that he was alcoholic, wasn't nearly as funny.

My first attempt at true seduction cooking happened when I was living with friends in a rambling old house near the University of Texas during my post-college years. Three of us shared plenty of meals, down-home foods with an Austin vibe: organic vegetarian one day, meaty Tex-Mex the next. I was working part time as a bank teller, and after weeks of flirting outrageously with Barry, a coworker, I invited him over for dinner. I remember mostly that I made a shrimp dish. The memory is clear because a package of shrimp (expensive to me, particularly in those days) was what I found on the floor, chewed up by our house's two kittens, about 20 minutes before my date was set to arrive.

Panicked, I convinced my housemate Doug to rush me to the nearest store to buy more, returning just in time to greet my date. I hurried through the making of the dish—curry something or other, I think—but I needn't have worried about the food, because Barry and I didn't even make it to the main course before the date, um, progressed. It said more about the fact that we were twenty-something men, with other priorities, than it did about any particular charms of the food.

Years later, a date with Juan, a beautiful-but-crazy Spanish-born Mexican, helped plant the seed for my food-journalism career, a seed that wouldn't sprout for almost a decade. I was living in Boston, and he had cooked a fantastic fish Veracruz for one of our first dates, all off the top of his head. When I tried to return the favor, Juan strode in, saw my kitchen in chaos, and announced that he had already eaten. Then he saw the stain-splattered *Silver Palate Good Times Cookbook* I had propped up on the counter, and laughed out loud. "Oh, how cute!" he said in his thick accent. "You have to use the cooking book!"

I was enraged. We didn't make it through our dinner either, but it wasn't because the date got ahead of itself. It was because I threw him out before we started.

. . .

After I went to culinary school and started writing about food, I had a particularly volatile relationship in Boston with Michael, whose favorite restaurant was my least—The Cheesecake Factory—even though I had never been there. ("Please," I would sniff. "Why would I go there?" Attractive, I know.) We argued over that and so many other things it's a wonder we ever got together, let alone dated for six months. We seemed to be always trying to prove something to each other, even as we were falling in love, or thought we were, or said we were.

Despite all the arguing, there were many affectionate moments, and I often think that if we had just been able to let each other be—and to maybe even let the other one "win" an argument from time to time—we could've even built a future together. When I cooked for Michael, he was always appreciative and complimentary, which says a lot. He also didn't seem to have many hangups about eating, unlike a date who exclaimed, "This is way too much food!" before I even put it on his plate and another who proclaimed that he doesn't "do" dessert, even though I had made it.

Our most memorable food connection was the time he tried to turn the tables on me. Michael lived in an apartment almost an hour outside Boston, right above his mother (one of the sticking points in our relationship). When he decided to cook for me, he wanted it to be at my place. But he didn't want me to watch, let alone help. "I'm going to come over Friday at six, and send you out for an hour while I make dinner," he said. "Go for a long walk with the dog."

I did, and when I came back the first thing I smelled was . . . well, not much of anything. He wouldn't let me in the kitchen (from which I heard no clanging of pots), but had set a place for me at the table. He brought out the first course, a romaine salad with very thick rings of red onions and

continued

· ·

pickled peperoncini on it. The entrée was beef roulade, stuffed with spinach and feta. There were slightly wrinkled green beans (or maybe it was slightly wrinkled new potatoes) on the side. The meat was tender and flavorful, and the side dish fine, but maybe not so fresh.

Michael grinned the entire time, and I have to say, I thought the endeavor was pretty charming, because I knew that he didn't usually cook. (He didn't have to: He had his mother.) Between bites, I started to realize that he was probably trying to prove a point again, and then it dawned on me what had happened.

When we finished, he couldn't wait a beat. "So," he asked, "what did you think? I did a pretty good job, didn't I? Maybe I can make something that's good enough even for you, right? And in only an hour!"

I know now what I should have said. I think about it from time to time, even still. In my mind I rewrite the scene. I pour a little more generosity into my heart and spirit, and I hear the guy I wish I had been able to be saying, "Honey, this was so delicious. Where'd you learn to make it? Can I get the recipe?" For all the food-Nazi snobbery I had espoused over the course of the relationship, including maligning his favorite restaurant, that better version of myself would have swallowed my pride and let him have his "gotcha" moment. In my revisionist fantasy, I would feign surprise when he told me the truth, the whole thing would dissolve into laughter and joy, and . . . scene.

Of course, that's not what I said. I was not that better me, so I said, with a smile, "I think you did an excellent job—of buying and reheating prepared food you got at Costco."

His face fell. "How did you know?"

"Well, I get paid to know such things," I said, then tried to backtrack. "But honestly, it was so sweet of you to make it, and it actually was good, and . . ."

The damage was done. "I can't believe you figured it out," he said. "I was so sure you'd be surprised."

Things were already shaky, but they went quickly downhill after that. After Michael and I broke up and some months passed, we got together, just as friends, to celebrate his birthday. I had a chance to make things up to him, at least a little bit.

I told him only that I was taking him to dinner and then to a show, but said nothing more. The show was a reading by David Sedaris, one of his favorite writers (and mine—something we could agree on!). For dinner beforehand, I suggested we meet in the Prudential Center mall, outside the Barnes & Noble. As we took the escalator down and passed all the people milling about on the stairs, holding their electronic beepers that would tell them when their table would be ready at the nearby Cheesecake Factory, Michael looked over at me, raised an eyebrow, and grinned.

The better version of me would have taken him there so much sooner.

· · ·

A couple of years ago I started seeing another food journalist, and by seeing I mean not actually seeing, as in laying my eyes on, but mainly talking about seeing because we live in different cities. It started as an *Up in the Air* kind of relationship, although (I think) without that part about one person lying about a spouse and children, and then it slowly progressed to something more. Or so I thought. When we got together, we'd devour food in one restaurant after another, in New Orleans, San Francisco, Montreal, and Atlanta. We had stimulating conversation about everything we ate (and we ate a hell of a lot), and we mostly agreed on what makes a dynamic, satisfying restaurant meal.

We were not souls colliding, it was neither volatile nor gothic, and I saw no train wreck in our future. Which seemed, well, perfect. Except for an unfortunate fact that I didn't learn until later: While I saw possibilities, he saw obstacles.

I should have known it was doomed when I realized that after a year of "seeing" each other, we had never eaten a home-cooked meal together. The truth is, the thought of cooking for him slightly terrified me, because deep down I knew that it represented a level of intimacy he wasn't prepared for.

Fast-forward to the writing of this book, and I've just started up something with another journalist, but this time someone who writes about politics, not food, and who enjoys a good meal as much as anyone but doesn't obsess about it. It's kind of refreshing, but who knows if it will last?

Yet again I'm faced with the prospect of the seduction meal. Will it happen? And if it does, what will I make? Already, I can't decide whether it will be more ridiculously fun to recreate the quail in rose petals from *Like Water For Chocolate*, to buy everything from the prepared-foods case at Costco, or to make one of my favorite single-serving dishes.

Doubled, of course.

INDEX

A

Almonds
Cherry-Almond Tart, 163
No-Bake Chocolate Oat
Cookies, 154
Spicy Almond Soba Noodles
with Edamame, 147
Wine-Braised Chicken Thighs
with Olives, Prunes, and
Almonds, 76
Yogurt Parfait with Mulled Red
Wine Syrup, Oranges, and
Almonds, 161
Apples
Pork Chop with Apples and
Brussels Sprouts, 68
Smoked Trout, Green Apple, and
Gouda Sandwich, 128
Arugula, Tuna, and Chickpea
Sandwich, 126
Asian pears
Cabbage and Pear Kimchi, 18
Korean Short Rib Tacos, 92–93
Asparagus, Tofu, and Farro Salad,
Charred, 144
Austin-Style Breakfast Tacos, 86
Avocados
Avocado-Chipotle Sauce, 48–49
Avocado, Smoked Oyster, and
Pistachio Bruschetta, 127
Black Bean Soup with Seared
Scallops and Green Salsa, 54
Chickpea, Spinach, Feta, and
Pepita Tacos, 89
Gingered Chicken Sandwich
with Avocado and Mango, 122
Mahi Mahi with Kiwi-Avocado
Salsa and Coconut Rice, 79
storing, 22
using leftover, 22

B

Bacon
Swiss Chard, Bacon, and Goat
Cheese Omelet, 34
Warm Spinach Salad with
Shiitakes, Corn, and Bacon,
56
Baked Egg in Fall Vegetables, 33
Bananas Foster, Coconut French
Toast with, 162
Basil, 21
Beans
Benedict Rancheros, 29
Black Bean Soup with Seared
Scallops and Green Salsa, 54
Black Bean Tortilla Soup with
Shrimp and Corn, 53
Chickpea, Spinach, Feta, and
Pepita Tacos, 89
dried, 47
Eggplant and Spicy Hummus
Flatbread, 115–16
Ex-Texas Salad, 51
Fall Vegetable Soup with White
Beans, 58
Farro Salad with Chickpeas,
Cherries, and Pecans, 143
Grapefruit–Black Bean
Salsa, 102
Home-Cooked Beans, 47
Peasant's Bowl, 50
Roasted Chile Relleno with
Avocado-Chipotle Sauce,
48–49
Spicy Almond Soba Noodles
with Edamame, 147
Spicy Black Bean Soup Base, 52
Spicy Hummus, 5
storing, 22
Sweet Potato Soup with Chorizo,
Chickpeas, and Kale, 43

Tuna, Chickpea, and Arugula
Sandwich, 126
using leftover, 22
Beef
chicken-fried steak, 60–61
Chili Cheese Enchiladas, 64
Korean Short Rib Tacos, 92–93
Pan-Fried Sirloin with Smashed
Potatoes and Anchovy
Sauce, 62
Spicy Glazed Mini Meatloaf, 65
Texas Bowl o' Red, 63
Beer
Texas Bowl o' Red, 63
Yucatan-Style Slow-Roasted
Pork, 66–67
Benedict Rancheros, 29
Black beans
Benedict Rancheros, 29
Black Bean Soup with Seared
Scallops and Green Salsa, 54
Black Bean Tortilla Soup with
Shrimp and Corn, 53
Ex-Texas Salad, 51
Grapefruit–Black Bean
Salsa, 102
Home-Cooked Beans, 47
Peasant's Bowl, 50
Roasted Chile Relleno with
Avocado-Chipotle Sauce,
48–49
Spicy Black Bean Soup Base, 52
storing, 22
using leftover, 22
Blackened Salsa, 16
Blueberries
Blueberry Lemon Jam, 10–11
Blueberry-Lemon Tart with
Toasted Coconut, 165
Bok Choy, Baby, Gingery Glazed
Halibut with Carrots and, 81

Bread. *See also* Sandwiches
  Avocado, Smoked Oyster, and
    Pistachio Bruschetta, 127
  Coconut French Toast with
    Bananas Foster, 162
  croutons, 120
  crumbs, 120
  Eggplant and Spicy Hummus
    Flatbread, 115–16
  storing, 120
  using leftover, 120
Broccolini
  Miso Pork on a Sweet Potato, 45
Broccoli rabe
  Philly-Style Chicken Cutlet
    Sandwich, 125

Broth, Corn, 3
Bruschetta, Avocado, Smoked
  Oyster, and Pistachio, 127
Brussels Sprouts, Pork Chop with
  Apples and, 68

C
Cabbage
  Cabbage and Pear Kimchi, 18
  Chipotle Slaw, 101
  Kimchi, Ham, and Fried Egg
    Pizza, 107
  Korean Short Rib Tacos, 92–93
Cantaloupe, Farfalle with
  Prosciutto and, 141
Cappuccino Tapioca Pudding with
  Cardamom Brûlée, 157
Cardamom–Brown Sugar
  Snickerdoodles, 153
Carrots, Gingery Glazed Halibut
  with Baby Bok Choy and, 81
Cashew Tamari Dressing, 7
Catfish Tacos with Chipotle
  Slaw, 101
Cauliflower
  Baked Egg in Fall Vegetables, 33

Fall Vegetable Soup with White
  Beans, 58
Fried Rice with Cauliflower and
  Kimchi, 136
Stewed Cauliflower, Butternut
  Squash, and Tomatoes, 55
Celery, 22
Charred Asparagus, Tofu, and
  Farro Salad, 144
Cheese
  Austin-Style Breakfast Tacos, 86
  Chickpea, Spinach, Feta, and
    Pepita Tacos, 89
  Chili Cheese Enchiladas, 64
  Ex-Texas Salad, 51
  Fig, Taleggio, and Radicchio
    Pizza, 111–12
  Miso Mac and Cheese with
    Mushrooms, 145
  Mushroom and Speck Pizza, 109
  Peasant's Bowl, 50
  Philly-Style Chicken Cutlet
    Sandwich, 125
  Roasted Chile Relleno with
    Avocado-Chipotle Sauce,
    48–49
  Shrimp Tacos with Grapefruit–
    Black Bean Salsa, 102
  Smoked Trout, Green Apple, and
    Gouda Sandwich, 128
  Smoked Turkey Tacos with Mole
    Verde, 96–97
  Smoky Pizza Margherita, 106
  Swiss Chard, Bacon, and Goat
    Cheese Omelet, 34
  Tacos with Mushrooms and
    Chile-Caramelized Onions, 88
  Texas Bowl o' Red, 63
  Three-Pepper Pizza with Goat
    Cheese, 118

Cherries
  Cherry-Almond Tart, 163
  Cornish Hen with Cherry-
    Hazelnut Wine Sauce, 77

Farro Salad with Chickpeas,
  Cherries, and Pecans, 143
No-Bake Chocolate Oat
  Cookies, 152
Chicken
  fresh vs. store-bought, 69–71
  Gingered Chicken Sandwich
    with Avocado and Mango, 122
  Philly-Style Chicken Cutlet
    Sandwich, 125
  Roast Chicken with Gremolata
    and Sunchokes, 72
  Wine-Braised Chicken Thighs
    with Olives, Prunes, and
    Almonds, 76
Chicken-fried steak, 60–61
Chickpeas
  Chickpea, Spinach, Feta, and
    Pepita Tacos, 89
  Eggplant and Spicy Hummus
    Flatbread, 115–16
  Farro Salad with Chickpeas,
    Cherries, and Pecans, 143
  Spicy Hummus, 5
  storing, 22
  Sweet Potato Soup with Chorizo,
    Chickpeas, and Kale, 43
  Tuna, Chickpea, and Arugula
    Sandwich, 126
  using leftover, 22
Chiles
  Habanero Salsa, 95
  Nam Pla Prik, 132
  Pickled Anchos, 20
  Roasted Chile Relleno with
    Avocado-Chipotle Sauce,
    48–49
  storing, 22, 23
  Texas Bowl o' Red, 63
  Three-Pepper Pizza with Goat
    Cheese, 118
  using leftover, 22, 23
Chili
  Chili Cheese Enchiladas, 64
  Texas Bowl o' Red, 63

Chocolate Oat Cookies,
No-Bake, 152
Chorizo
Austin-Style Breakfast Tacos, 86
Sweet Potato Soup with Chorizo,
Chickpeas, and Kale, 43
Chutney, Red Pepper, 17
Cilantro
Cilantro Vinaigrette, 9
Green Mango Slaw, 121
Mole Verde Sauce, 96
Salsa Verde, 14
storing, 21
using leftover, 21
Citrus-Pickled Onions, 19
Cochinita Pibil Tacos with
Habanero Salsa, 95
Coconut milk and coconut water
Coconut French Toast with
Bananas Foster, 162
Curried Shrimp on a Sweet
Potato, 46
Mahi Mahi with Kiwi-Avocado
Salsa and Coconut Rice, 79
Spicy Coconut Sorbet, 159
storing, 23
using leftover, 23
Confit, Herbed Lemon, 4
Cookies
Cardamom–Brown Sugar
Snickerdoodles, 153
No-Bake Chocolate Oat
Cookies, 152
Pistachio Butter Cookies, 154–55
Corn. See also Tortillas (corn)
Black Bean Tortilla Soup with
Shrimp and Corn, 53
Corn Broth, 3
Corn Risotto with Roasted
Cherry Tomatoes, 135
Warm Spinach Salad with
Shiitakes, Corn, and
Bacon, 56

Cornish hen
Cornish Hen with Cherry-
Hazelnut Wine Sauce, 77
Pineapple-Juice-Can Hen and
Baby Potatoes, 74–75
Couscous, Turbot with Tomatoes,
Walnuts, and Capers over, 80
Croutons, 120
Curried Butternut Squash
Risotto, 137
Curried Shrimp on a Sweet
Potato, 46

D

Desserts
Blueberry-Lemon Tart with
Toasted Coconut, 165
Cappuccino Tapioca Pudding
with Cardamom Brûlée, 157
Cardamom–Brown Sugar
Snickerdoodles, 153
Cherry-Almond Tart, 163
Coconut French Toast with
Bananas Foster, 162
Hibiscus-Poached Peach, 158
No-Bake Chocolate Oat
Cookies, 152
Pistachio Butter Cookies, 154–55
Spicy Coconut Sorbet, 159
Yogurt Parfait with Mulled Red
Wine Syrup, Oranges, and
Almonds, 161
Yogurt Parfait with Rhubarb-
Ginger Sauce and
Strawberries, 160
Duck Breast Tacos with Plum
Salsa, 99–100
Duck Egg Frittata, Puffy, with
Smoked Salmon, 36

E

Edamame, Spicy Almond Soba
Noodles with, 147

Eggplant and Spicy Hummus
Flatbread, 115–16
Eggs
Austin-Style Breakfast Tacos, 86
Baked Egg in Fall Vegetables, 33
Benedict Rancheros, 29
hard-cooked, 31
Kimchi, Ham, and Fried Egg
Pizza, 107–8
Low, Slow, and Custardy
Eggs, 30
Mushroom and Green Garlic
Frittata, 32
nutrition and, 27
poached, 31
Puffy Duck Egg Frittata with
Smoked Salmon, 36
Shrimp and Potato Chip
Tortilla, 35
Swiss Chard, Bacon, and Goat
Cheese Omelet, 34
Tacos de Huevos, 87
Thai Fried Rice with Runny Egg,
132–33
Tuna, Egg, and Potato Salad
Sandwich, 123
Enchiladas, Chili Cheese, 64
Ex-Texas Salad, 51

F

Fall Vegetable Soup with White
Beans, 58
Farfalle with Cantaloupe and
Prosciutto, 141
Farro
Charred Asparagus, Tofu, and
Farro Salad, 144
Farro Salad with Chickpeas,
Cherries, and Pecans, 143
making, 143
Roasted Chile Relleno with
Avocado-Chipotle Sauce,
48–49

Faux-Lognese with Pappardelle, 140

Fedelini with Tuna Ragu, 148

Fennel
Fideos with Sardines and Bread Crumbs, 149
Red Pepper Chutney, 17
Smoked Trout, Potato, and Fennel Pizza, 113–14
storing, 22
using leftover, 22

Fideos with Sardines and Bread Crumbs, 149

Fig, Taleggio, and Radicchio Pizza, 111–12

Fish
Catfish Tacos with Chipotle Slaw, 101
Fedelini with Tuna Ragu, 148
Fideos with Sardines and Bread Crumbs, 149
Gingery Glazed Halibut with Carrots and Baby Bok Choy, 81
Mahi Mahi with Kiwi-Avocado Salsa and Coconut Rice, 79
Puffy Duck Egg Frittata with Smoked Salmon, 36
Smoked Trout, Green Apple, and Gouda Sandwich, 128
Smoked Trout, Potato, and Fennel Pizza, 113–14
Turbot with Tomatoes, Walnuts, and Capers over Couscous, 80

Flatbread, Eggplant and Spicy Hummus, 115–16

French Toast, Coconut, with Bananas Foster, 162

Fried Rice with Cauliflower and Kimchi, 136

Frittatas
Mushroom and Green Garlic Frittata, 32

Puffy Duck Egg Frittata with Smoked Salmon, 36

G

Garlic
Mushroom and Green Garlic Frittata, 32
Parsley Garlic Dressing, 8

Gingered Chicken Sandwich with Avocado and Mango, 122

Gingery Glazed Halibut with Carrots and Baby Bok Choy, 81

Grapefruit
Citrus-Pickled Onions, 19
Grapefruit–Black Bean Salsa, 102

Green Mango Slaw, 121

Gremolata, 72

Guinea hen
Cornish Hen with Cherry-Hazelnut Wine Sauce, 77
Pineapple-Juice-Can Hen and Baby Potatoes, 74–75

H

Habanero Salsa, 95

Halibut, Gingery Glazed, with Carrots and Baby Bok Choy, 81

Ham
Farfalle with Cantaloupe and Prosciutto, 141
Kimchi, Ham, and Fried Egg Pizza, 107–8
Hazelnut-Cherry Wine Sauce, Cornish Hen with, 77

Herbs. *See also individual herbs*
Herbed Lemon Confit, 4
storing, 21
using leftover, 21

Hibiscus-Poached Peach, 158

Home-Cooked Beans, 47

Homemade Corn Tortillas, 84–85

Hummus
Eggplant and Spicy Hummus Flatbread, 115–16
Spicy Hummus, 5

J

Jams
Blueberry Lemon Jam, 10–11
Strawberry Vanilla Jam, 12–13

K

Kale, Sweet Potato Soup with Chorizo, Chickpeas, and, 43

Kimchi
Cabbage and Pear Kimchi, 18
Fried Rice with Cauliflower and Kimchi, 136

Kimchi, Ham, and Fried Egg Pizza, 107–8

Kiwi-Avocado Salsa, 79

Korean Short Rib Tacos, 92–93

L

Lemons
Blueberry Lemon Jam, 10–11
Blueberry-Lemon Tart with Toasted Coconut, 165
Herbed Lemon Confit, 4

Limes
Black Bean Soup with Seared Scallops and Green Salsa, 54
Citrus-Pickled Onions, 19
storing, 21
using leftover, 21

Low, Slow, and Custardy Eggs, 30

M

Mac and Cheese with Mushrooms, Miso, 145

Mahi Mahi with Kiwi-Avocado Salsa and Coconut Rice, 79

Mangoes
Gingered Chicken Sandwich with Avocado and Mango, 124
Green Mango Slaw, 121

Meatloaf, Spicy Glazed Mini, 65

Mint, 21

Miso
Miso Mac and Cheese with Mushrooms, 145
Miso Pork on a Sweet Potato, 45

Mole Verde Sauce, 96

Mulled Wine Syrup, 6

Mushrooms
Miso Mac and Cheese with Mushrooms, 145
Mushroom and Green Garlic Frittata, 32
Mushroom and Speck Pizza, 109
Tacos with Mushrooms and Chile-Caramelized Onions, 88
Thai Fried Rice with Runny Egg, 132–33
Warm Spinach Salad with Shiitakes, Corn, and Bacon, 56

N

Nam Pla Prik, 132

No-Bake Chocolate Oat Cookies, 152

No-Knead Pizza Dough, 104

No-Knead Pizza Dough with Spelt, 105

Noodles. See Pasta and noodles

O

Oat Cookies, No-Bake Chocolate, 152

Olives, Wine-Braised Chicken Thighs with Prunes, Almonds, and, 76

Omelet, Swiss Chard, Bacon, and Goat Cheese, 34

Onions
Citrus-Pickled Onions, 19
Tacos with Mushrooms and Chile-Caramelized Onions, 88

Oranges
Citrus-Pickled Onions, 19
Sweet Potato and Orange Soup with Smoky Pecans, 44
Yogurt Parfait with Mulled Red Wine Syrup, Oranges, and Almonds, 161
Yucatan-Style Slow-Roasted Pork, 66–67

Oyster, Smoked, Avocado, and Pistachio Bruschetta, 127

P

Paella, Personal, with Squid and Scallions, 139

Pan-Fried Sirloin with Smashed Potatoes and Anchovy Sauce, 62

Parfaits
Yogurt Parfait with Mulled Red Wine Syrup, Oranges, and Almonds, 161
Yogurt Parfait with Rhubarb-Ginger Sauce and Strawberries, 160

Parsley
Gremolata, 72
Parsley Garlic Dressing, 8
storing, 21
using leftover, 21

Pasta and noodles
Farfalle with Cantaloupe and Prosciutto, 141
Faux-Lognese with Pappardelle, 140
Fedelini with Tuna Ragu, 148
Fideos with Sardines and Bread Crumbs, 149
Miso Mac and Cheese with Mushrooms, 145
Spicy Almond Soba Noodles with Edamame, 147

Pastoral Tacos, 91

Peach, Hibiscus-Poached, 158

Peasant's Bowl, 50

Pecans
Coconut French Toast with Bananas Foster, 162
Farro Salad with Chickpeas, Cherries, and Pecans, 143
Sweet Potato and Orange Soup with Smoky Pecans, 44

Pepitas. See Pumpkin seeds

Peppers. See also Chiles
Curried Shrimp on a Sweet Potato, 46
Philly-Style Chicken Cutlet Sandwich, 125
Red Pepper Chutney, 17
Three-Pepper Pizza with Goat Cheese, 118

Personal Paella with Squid and Scallions, 139

Philly-Style Chicken Cutlet Sandwich, 125

Pickled Anchos, 20

Pineapple
Pastoral Tacos, 91
Pineapple-Juice-Can Hen and Baby Potatoes, 74–75

Pistachios
Avocado, Smoked Oyster, and Pistachio Bruschetta, 127
Curried Butternut Squash Risotto, 137
Pistachio Butter Cookies, 154–55

Pizzas
broiling, 108
Fig, Taleggio, and Radicchio Pizza, 111–12

Kimchi, Ham, and Fried Egg
    Pizza, 107
Mushroom and Speck Pizza, 109
No-Knead Pizza Dough, 104
No-Knead Pizza Dough with
    Spelt, 105
Smoked Trout, Potato, and
    Fennel Pizza, 113–14
Smoky Pizza Margherita, 106
Three-Pepper Pizza with Goat
    Cheese, 118
Plum Salsa, 99–100
Pork
    Cochinita Pibil Tacos with
        Habanero Salsa, 95
    Faux-Lognese with
        Pappardelle, 140
    Miso Pork on a Sweet Potato, 45
    Pastoral Tacos, 91
    Pork Chop with Apples and
        Brussels Sprouts, 68
    Pulled Pork Sandwich with
        Green Mango Slaw, 121
    Yucatan-Style Slow-Roasted
        Pork, 66–67
Potato Chip and Shrimp Tortilla, 35
Potatoes
    Austin-Style Breakfast Tacos, 86
    Pan-Fried Sirloin with
        Smashed Potatoes and
        Anchovy Sauce, 62
    Pineapple-Juice-Can Hen and
        Baby Potatoes, 74–75
    Smoked Trout, Potato, and
        Fennel Pizza, 113–14
    Tuna, Egg, and Potato Salad
        Sandwich, 123
Prosciutto, Farfalle with
    Cantaloupe and, 141
Prunes, Wine-Braised Chicken
    Thighs with Olives, Almonds,
    and, 76
Pudding, Cappuccino Tapioca,
    with Cardamom Brûlée, 157

Puff pastry
    Blueberry-Lemon Tart with
        Toasted Coconut, 165
    Cherry-Almond Tart, 163
Puffy Duck Egg Frittata with
    Smoked Salmon, 36
Pulled Pork Sandwich with Green
    Mango Slaw, 121
Pumpkin seeds
    Chickpea, Spinach, Feta, and
        Pepita Tacos, 89
    Mole Verde Sauce, 96
    roasting, 89, 97

R
Radicchio, Fig, and Taleggio Pizza,
    111–12
Red Pepper Chutney, 17
Restaurant dining, 24–25
Rhubarb-Ginger Sauce, 160
Rice
    Corn Risotto with Roasted
        Cherry Tomatoes, 135
    Curried Butternut Squash
        Risotto, 137
    Fried Rice with Cauliflower and
        Kimchi, 136
    Mahi Mahi with Kiwi-Avocado
        Salsa and Coconut Rice, 79
    Peasant's Bowl, 50
    Personal Paella with Squid and
        Scallions, 139
    Roasted Chile Relleno with
        Avocado-Chipotle Sauce,
        48–49
    Thai Fried Rice with Runny Egg,
        132–33
Risotto
    Corn Risotto with Roasted
        Cherry Tomatoes, 135
    Curried Butternut Squash
        Risotto, 137
Roast Chicken with Gremolata and
    Sunchokes, 72

Roasted Chile Relleno with
    Avocado-Chipotle Sauce,
    48–49

S
Salad dressings
    Cashew Tamari Dressing, 7
    Cilantro Vinaigrette, 9
    Parsley Garlic Dressing, 8
Salads
    Charred Asparagus, Tofu, and
        Farro Salad, 144
    Chipotle Slaw, 101
    Ex-Texas Salad, 51
    Farro Salad with Chickpeas,
        Cherries, and Pecans, 143
    Green Mango Slaw, 121
    Tuna, Egg, and Potato Salad
        Sandwich, 123
    Warm Spinach Salad
        with Shiitakes, Corn,
        and Bacon, 56
Salmon, Smoked, Puffy Duck Egg
    Frittata with, 36
Salsas. See Sauces and salsas
Sandwiches
    Gingered Chicken Sandwich
        with Avocado and Mango, 122
    Philly-Style Chicken Cutlet
        Sandwich, 125
    Pulled Pork Sandwich with
        Green Mango Slaw, 121
    Smoked Trout, Green Apple, and
        Gouda Sandwich, 128
    Tuna, Chickpea, and Arugula
        Sandwich, 126
    Tuna, Egg, and Potato Salad
        Sandwich, 123
Sardines, Fideos with Bread
    Crumbs and, 149
Sauces and salsas
    Avocado-Chipotle Sauce, 48–49
    Blackened Salsa, 16
    Cherry-Hazelnut Wine Sauce, 77

Sauces and salsas, *continued*
  Grapefruit–Black Bean
    Salsa, 102
  Green Salsa, 54
  Habanero Salsa, 95
  Kiwi-Avocado Salsa, 79
  Mole Verde Sauce, 96
  Nam Pla Prik, 134
  Plum Salsa, 99–100
  Rhubarb-Ginger Sauce, 160
  Salsa Verde, 14
Scallops, Seared, Black Bean Soup
    with Green Salsa and, 54
Shopping tips, 40
Shrimp
  Black Bean Tortilla Soup with
    Shrimp and Corn, 53
  Curried Shrimp on a Sweet
    Potato, 46
  Shrimp and Potato Chip
    Tortilla, 35
  Shrimp Tacos with Grapefruit–
    Black Bean Salsa, 102
Slaws
  Chipotle Slaw, 101
  Green Mango Slaw, 121
Smoked Trout, Green Apple, and
    Gouda Sandwich, 128
Smoked Trout, Potato, and Fennel
    Pizza, 113–14
Smoked Turkey Tacos with Mole
    Verde, 96–97
Smoky Pizza Margherita, 106
Snickerdoodles, Cardamom–
    Brown Sugar, 153
Soba Noodles, Spicy Almond, with
    Edamame, 147
Sorbet, Spicy Coconut, 159
Soups
  Black Bean Soup with Seared
    Scallops and Green Salsa, 54
  Black Bean Tortilla Soup with
    Shrimp and Corn, 53
  Fall Vegetable Soup with White
    Beans, 58

Spicy Black Bean Soup Base, 52
Sweet Potato and Orange Soup
    with Smoky Pecans, 44
Sweet Potato Soup Base, 41
Sweet Potato Soup with Chorizo,
    Chickpeas, and Kale, 43
Speck and Mushroom Pizza, 109
Spelt, No-Knead Pizza Dough
    with, 105
Spicy Almond Soba Noodles with
    Edamame, 147
Spicy Black Bean Soup Base, 52
Spicy Coconut Sorbet, 159
Spicy Glazed Mini Meatloaf, 65
Spicy Hummus, 5
Spinach
  Chickpea, Spinach, Feta, and
    Pepita Tacos, 89
  Warm Spinach Salad
    with Shiitakes, Corn,
    and Bacon, 56
Squash
  Baked Egg in Fall Vegetables, 33
  Curried Butternut Squash
    Risotto, 137
  Fall Vegetable Soup with White
    Beans, 58
  Stewed Cauliflower, Butternut
    Squash, and Tomatoes, 55
Squid, Personal Paella with
    Scallions and, 139
Stewed Cauliflower, Butternut
    Squash, and Tomatoes, 55
Storage tips, 21–23
Strawberries
  Strawberry Vanilla Jam, 12–13
  Yogurt Parfait with Rhubarb-
    Ginger Sauce and
    Strawberries, 160
Sunchokes, Roast Chicken with
    Gremolata and, 72
Sweet potatoes
  Curried Shrimp on a Sweet
    Potato, 46
  Miso Pork on a Sweet Potato, 45

Sweet Potato and Orange Soup
    with Smoky Pecans, 44
Sweet Potato Soup Base, 41
Sweet Potato Soup with Chorizo,
    Chickpeas, and Kale, 43
Tacos de Huevos, 87
Swiss chard
  Roasted Chile Relleno with
    Avocado-Chipotle Sauce,
    48–49
  Swiss Chard, Bacon, and Goat
    Cheese Omelet, 34
Syrup, Mulled Wine, 6

T

Tacos
  Austin-Style Breakfast Tacos, 86
  Catfish Tacos with Chipotle
    Slaw, 101
  Chickpea, Spinach, Feta, and
    Pepita Tacos, 89
  Cochinita Pibil Tacos with
    Habanero Salsa, 95
  Duck Breast Tacos with Plum
    Salsa, 99–100
  Korean Short Rib Tacos, 92–93
  Pastoral Tacos, 91
  Shrimp Tacos with Grapefruit–
    Black Bean Salsa, 102
  Smoked Turkey Tacos with Mole
    Verde, 96–97
  Tacos de Huevos, 87
  Tacos with Mushrooms and
    Chile-Caramelized Onions, 88
Tapioca Pudding, Cappuccino,
    with Cardamom Brûlée, 157
Tarts
  Blueberry-Lemon Tart with
    Toasted Coconut, 165
  Cherry-Almond Tart, 163
Texas Bowl o' Red, 63
Thai Fried Rice with Runny Egg,
    132–33

Three-Pepper Pizza with Goat
     Cheese, 118
Thyme, 21
Tofu
   Charred Asparagus, Tofu, and
      Farro Salad, 146
   Parsley Garlic Dressing, 8
Tomatillos
   Black Bean Soup with Seared
      Scallops and Green Salsa, 54
   Mole Verde Sauce, 96
   Salsa Verde, 14
Tomatoes
   Baked Egg in Fall Vegetables, 33
   Benedict Rancheros, 29
   Black Bean Tortilla Soup with
      Shrimp and Corn, 53
   Blackened Salsa, 16
   Chickpea, Spinach, Feta, and
      Pepita Tacos, 89
   Corn Risotto with Roasted
      Cherry Tomatoes, 135
   Ex-Texas Salad, 51
   Fall Vegetable Soup with White
      Beans, 58
   Farro Salad with Chickpeas,
      Cherries, and Pecans, 143
   Faux Lognese with Pappardelle,
      140
   Fedelini with Tuna Ragu, 148
   Peasant's Bowl, 50
   Roasted Chile Relleno with
      Avocado-Chipotle Sauce,
      48–49
   Smoky Pizza Margherita, 108
   Stewed Cauliflower, Butternut
      Squash, and Tomatoes, 55
   storing, 23
   Thai Fried Rice with Runny Egg,
      132–33
   Turbot with Tomatoes,
      Walnuts, and Capers
      over Couscous, 80
   12-Hour Tomatoes, 2
   using leftover, 23

Tortilla (egg), Shrimp and Potato
      Chip, 35
Tortillas (corn)
   Black Bean Tortilla Soup with
      Shrimp and Corn, 53
   Catfish Tacos with Chipotle
      Slaw, 101
   Chickpea, Spinach, Feta, and
      Pepita Tacos, 89
   Chili Cheese Enchiladas, 64
   Cochinita Pibil Tacos with
      Habanero Salsa, 95
   Duck Breast Tacos with Plum
      Salsa, 99–100
   Ex-Texas Salad, 51
   Homemade Corn Tortillas, 84–85
   Korean Short Rib Tacos, 92–93
   Pastoral Tacos, 91
   Shrimp Tacos with Grapefruit–
      Black Bean Salsa, 102
   Smoked Turkey Tacos with Mole
      Verde, 96–97
   Tacos de Huevos, 87
   Tacos with Mushrooms and
      Chile-Caramelized Onions, 88
   working with, 85
Tortillas (flour)
   Austin-Style Breakfast Tacos, 86

Trout
   Smoked Trout, Green Apple, and
      Gouda Sandwich, 128
   Smoked Trout, Potato, and
      Fennel Pizza, 113–14
Tuna
   Fedelini with Tuna Ragu, 148
   Tuna, Chickpea, and Arugula
      Sandwich, 126
   Tuna, Egg, and Potato Salad
      Sandwich, 123
Turbot with Tomatoes,
      Walnuts, and Capers
      over Couscous, 80
Turkey Tacos, Smoked, with Mole
   Verde, 96–97

12-Hour Tomatoes, 2
Two, cooking for, 166–69

V

Vinaigrettes. See Salad dressings

W

Walnuts
   Fig, Taleggio, and Radicchio
      Pizza, 111–12
   Turbot with Tomatoes,
      Walnuts, and Capers
      over Couscous, 80
Warm Spinach Salad with
      Shiitakes, Corn, and
      Bacon, 56
Wine
   Cornish Hen with Cherry-
      Hazelnut Wine Sauce, 77
   Mulled Wine Syrup, 6
   storing, 23
   using leftover, 23
   Wine-Braised Chicken Thighs
      with Olives, Prunes, and
      Almonds, 76
Woks, 136

Y

Yogurt
   Yogurt Parfait with Mulled Red
      Wine Syrup, Oranges, and
      Almonds, 161
   Yogurt Parfait with Rhubarb-
      Ginger Sauce and
      Strawberries, 160
Yucatan-Style Slow-Roasted Pork,
   66–67

ABOUT THE AUTHOR

The former travel editor at the *Boston Globe*, **JOE YONAN** is currently the food and travel editor at *The Washington Post*, where he writes the award-winning "Cooking for One" column. Joe's work also earned the *Post* the 2009 and 2010 James Beard Foundation's award for best food section.